D1744051

PSYCHOLOGY & THE CITY:

THE HIDDEN DIMENSION

BY CHARLES LANDRY
& CHRIS MURRAY

COMEDIA

08

First published by Comedia in the UK in 2017

ISBN: 978-1-908777-07-2

Comedia The Round, Bournes Green Near Stroud, GL6 7NL, UK

Book design: **www.hillsdesign.co.uk**

All photographs: **Charles Landry**

Cover photograph: *The experience of our world is refracted in multiple ways.*

Charles Landry has for 35 years attempted to shift how we think about the potential of cities and what their tangible and intangible resources can be starting with the concept of the Creative City in the late 1980's. This focuses on how cities can create the conditions to think, plan and act with imagination. Later he explored the sensory landscape of cities and how the art and science of cities can come together.

Chris Murray is currently Director of the Core Cities UK, is a visiting Professor of Practice at Newcastle University, an Honorary Fellow of the Heseltine Institute at Liverpool University, and Chair of award winning social enterprise business group Fusion 21. He was previously a Director of the Commission for Architecture and the Built Environment, and worked for the UK Deputy Prime Minister to establish the Academy for Sustainable Communities, a national regeneration skills agency. He previously worked in psychiatry.

RECYCLED
Paper made from
recycled material
FSC
www.fsc.org   FSC® C007326

Printed on FSC® certified paper, using fully sustainable, vegetable oil-based inks, power from 100% renewable resources and waterless printing technology.

Tainan: Widening a boulevard cut houses in half and led to protests. Artists repainted what had been there.

CONTENTS

*Umea: Exhibition
in the Bildmuseet
by Thilo Frank. We
reflect the city and
the city reflects us.*

AIMS AND INTENT

"What is the city but the people" *Shakespeare's Coriolanus*

"We shape our buildings; thereafter they shape us." *Winston Churchill*

"It is ironic that we know more about the habitat of mountain gorillas than we do about the habitat of people." *Jan Gehl*

Being in a city is a two-way psychological process. The city impacts upon our mind – our mental and emotional state impacts upon the city. This is part of a constant cycle of influencing and being influenced, perpetual transactions changing moment to moment as our daily lived experience unfolds, with repercussions both for us and for the city in ways we cannot always be aware of. Revealing these interactions and their impacts is important in understanding how we can make, manage and inhabit places.

To see the urban fabric, its forms, its dynamics and city life as empty shells devoid of human psychological content is careless. To be blind to its consequences is foolish, because in a significant sense the city is primarily an emotional experience with psychological effects.

It is astonishing then that psychology, the area of study that explores the dynamics of feeling and emotion, has not been taken sufficiently seriously as an urban discipline, by psychology itself but also by urban decision makers, since it seeks to understand why we act the way we do. Crucially the personal psychological dispositions and mindsets of those who shape cities also determine our urban life, hopefully to improve our overall wellbeing and resilience, for us to mature, deal with adversity and live fulfilling lives. We might also ask how a city develops a psychology of its own, is it more masculine or feminine, nurturing or self-centred, introvert or extrovert. Psychology concerns itself with individuals, organisations and groups, but – with notable exceptions – not the city.

The city is not a lifeless thing. People have personality, identity and, as they are congregations of people, so do cities. The 'urban psyche' could be described as the complex personality that emerges from the interactions between people and place. Urban psychology is the evolving science of understanding more about this urban psyche alongside our own psychological response to cities, and is about how we can use that knowledge to effect how cities are shaped.

Rather than setting out a definite and fixed position, in this short book our intent is to help embed psychological knowledge into city-making and to open up a new conversation and stimulate thinking, through the following.

• Outlining why urban psychology is important now.

• Describing the potential of different schools of psychology to better understanding cities and their citizens.

The city is not a lifeless thing. People have personality, identity... and so do cities.

• Highlighting how as a species we have only recently become a 'homo urbanis' and how deep-seated yearnings and visceral instincts from our long-lost past still condition our reactions to modern circumstances.

• Exploring whether cities can have a deeper sense of psyche and 'soul' – we often describe places as 'soulless'.

• Describing how we might measure the psychological pulse of a city, and what this can mean for those responsible for making cities work.

• Outlining briefly the results in eleven cities from our City Personality Test.

• Sketching out a toolkit for the Psychologically Resilient City, and suggesting 'where next'.

The city powerfully affects our motivations, habits and behaviour, which in turn determine the success or failure of our projects and programmes, of our city making in general, and also how a city feels. Consider simply how ugly places generate a sense of hopelessness and lack of care, or how ones seen as more beautiful can lift energies. Understanding the psychology of places is a vital missing thread in urban thinking and will help us create better cities more in tune with our deeper feelings and needs.

Venice Guggenheim: The flourescent tubes by
Maurizio Nannucci resonate well the changing world

WHY WE NEED URBAN PSYCHOLOGY NOW

'Psychology & the City' is the latest step in an evolving long-term endeavour to reshape city making and to shift its intellectual architecture.

This started 25 years ago, by connecting creativity, culture and the city together as the driving forces in cities' adaptation to change and reinvention: The Creative City project. The culture of a place, its origins, its history, its location, its resources, we noted, is etched into and shapes how a city acts, determining its prospects. Creativity is a unique capacity and source for imagining what a city can become, helping us identify, nurture, harness, exploit and promote its values and assets. How creative a place can be is determined partly by its culture, and its culture is determined by its psychology.

We then re-emphasized that the city is not just a machine but more a living organism existing within a sensory landscape where a rich register of emotions is triggered by how it looks and feels. We challenged cities to assess and plan themselves simultaneously through a 'hardware and software' lens, giving equal weighting to measurements concerned with peoples' lived experience of place and not only those concerned with hard infrastructure or economics. This step brought together the cultural sectors and social sciences.

Seeing the city through psychological lens is the next step, and an urgent one, as the complexity of issues affecting cities is accelerating, threatening to overwhelm our current policy toolkit. The world is now predominantly urban with cities growing at a breath-taking pace as 1.5 million people each week move to cities (roughly 200,000+ a day or 140 every minute).

There are threats to urban stability like climate change, crises of food and energy security, health problems and ageing, intercultural living, resource constraints, poverty and inequality. Concerns over economic inequality were shown in one global survey to "trump all other dangers"[1], and are now an influence in the rise of anti-

Taipei: A small skyscraper as a totem pole – an archetypal symbol of identity and belonging which overpowers its ugly neighbours

establishment, populist and nationalist movements, which can in turn play on deep-seated psychological fears. Such movements are often critical of cities, perhaps exactly because they tend to be more open and liberal. Difference is an everyday thing in cities and tolerant places just feel easier to live in.

Strained finances limit cities ability to deal with these issues, but it is not just about more resource. An understanding of the psychological dynamics that are at play for individuals and groups can help us towards new solutions that focus the available resources in the most effective way possible. Urban psychology could in this way have a profound economic and public-service impact. Economics itself has been described as a branch of psychology.

... understanding the psychological dynamics at play for individuals can help create better urban solutions

A growing population exerts pressure on everything and the mass movement of people across the globe can impact on urban identities dramatically if not properly managed. The effects of this density of people can burst out in unexpected and explosive ways. Our inability to grasp these risks and how to deal with them can create intense governance, management but also psychological problems.

Internationally, concerns are rising over mental health, and the percentages of people experiencing mental health issues is far higher in cities, alongside evidence that the bigger the city, the greater the likely mental health impacts[1]. The reasons for this are complex and closely linked to poverty, but also to overcrowding, excessive noise and bland, soulless environments. There is also a greater awareness of the socio-economic impacts of mental health. For example, we cannot forget that every suicide is first and foremost a human tragedy, but neither should we ignore the fact that the total cost of someone jumping under a train is around £2 million[2]. Prevention is far cheaper than crisis, and by applying a psychological lens to the city, we can reduce its worst mental health impacts and accentuate its best.

Overlaid on this are the delights and discontents of digitization. The ability to be constantly connected, to be 'here and there' simultaneously; the blending of 'real' and virtual worlds can break focus and fragment our attention. In a more nomadic world the sense of belonging linked to place can disperse across networks and geographical boundaries. It can change our conception of

Southwold: The mass of cars everywhere can overwhelm

space, place and time, affecting how we relate to the city. Add to this the new disruptive technologies such as artificial intelligence or sensing systems and world feels as if it is on a rollercoaster.

Cities are places where most of us are strangers. They are a mix of people with intensely personal histories, differing cultures and perspectives, views of life and interests who have come together to share a collective space. But cities are also the spatial-level par excellence for uniting diverse identities into a common whole, places where face-to-face interaction still really matters as a means of binding and bonding people, building a sense of shared community, citizenship, and stewardship of place.

Revealing and then working with the composite character or psychology of a city can be a powerful tool in understanding what pushes a place forwards or holds it back, what curtails or contributes to its civic life, what creates the spirit of a place and how that embeds itself into attitudes and organisational cultures, determining its future.

The Hidden Dimension

Urban psychology is a way of making visible the hidden patterns and unseen drivers shaping cities. By putting psychology onto the urban agenda, we aim to reinforce and affirm the significance of subjective experience. It is the combination of quantitative measures, such as location, economic assets or history, and our personal qualitative

Macau: Are people walking away from such intense density

responses that shape what cities as collective entities are able to do and their achievements. Few would argue that understanding human behaviour is crucial, nor that psychology is an important discipline.

It is endlessly noted that we live in an urban age and attempts to understand our evolution to 'homo urbanis', a predominantly urban species, are underway across many disciplines: sociology, anthropology, ethnography, geography, politics, environmental science, economics, design and culture. Researchers have looked at the built environment, energy consumption and pollution, food supply and security, health in cities from obesity to depression, movement and mobility, demographics and ageing, and urban agglomeration economics.

We have only been an urban species for a short time.

This research provides a growing awareness of the fragility of cities, the risk nexus of escalating vulnerabilities and stresses in a world of remorseless change. Interconnected global challenges are growing in scale and scope in a way that affects cities directly and demands behaviour change.

How can you understand behaviour change or global transitions without understanding psychology? This curious omission is worrying. Is it because we are scared to face ourselves and our emotions? Is it the training of those running cities, who feel they need to appear rational, logical and sober and think psychology is vague? Unfolding events in cities that at first sight may seem illogical can be unscrambled and interpreted by looking at the range of psychological responses people display.

What comes first, history, culture or is it landscape, location or resources that determine a city's destiny? Is it the chicken or the egg? There are complex relationships between these factors and most have been credited with strong explanatory value. All these circumstances etch themselves into the urban psyche, influencing the culture of place.

Bold attempts to bring psychological disciplines to bear on the urban condition have been and continue to be made, which we applaud. But so far these have been limited and are – relative to other research interests – in their urban infancy[3].

Does history, culture or psychology or landscape, location or resources come first in shaping a city's destiny?

We have now conducted primary research with eleven cities through a 'City Personality Test', detailed in Chapter 8. Although further research is needed, this has produced valuable insights and has led to a new kind of discussion about cities as diverse as Adelaide, Bilbao, Milton Keynes, Minneapolis, Ghent, Antwerp, Krakow, Plymouth, Oslo and Mannheim. Decision makers were surprised at the depth of insight and help they received through using the Test as a jumping-off point in moving forward with their city and in creating a new strategic conversation about their future. The Test is about individual perceptions of a city's residents or users. It is their reality, not necessarily the reality of the place or a scientific evaluation, yet the results suggest it correlates well with the local reality.

CITIES AND THEIR PSYCHOLOGY: EXAMPLES AND IMPACT

Some cities we call sober, others constrained, thwarted, stifling and reduced or edgy, 'can do' and open or welcoming, among many other adjectives.

These **can be described as personality traits both in humans and cities.** Our responses to geography, location, resources and weather can all shape this sense of personality. Contrast the demeanour, attitudes and behaviours of someone from a colder northern city to a person living on the equator. The difference between port cities and those inland, in mountains or on the plains. Think of a capital city or a satellite. Citizens of different places are perceived as arrogant, vibrant, self-important or subdued. Physical environments too have differing effects. Places perceived as ugly, with endless swathes of asphalt and the ever-present noise and smell of cars can drain the spirit. This can enclose people and make them anxious and uncommunicative. At the other extreme, places seen as beautiful can lift the senses and engender a feeling that the world is in order or stable and so strengthen confidence and open people up. This yearning for wholeness is powerful. Can these factors curtail city ambition and prospects? Urban atmospheres differ sharply as does a sense of confidence, and we need to ask what is its deeper source.

We have a good understanding of how places work in many respects, for example socially, economically or via the ramifications of urban design. But we are far less experienced at tapping into the deeper layers of urban life that may reveal hidden dynamics, that can have a causal relationship to success or failure. Without this knowledge, we often interpret outcomes as unexpected or as unintended consequences. At Comedia we have been measuring some of these dynamics by looking at the creative capacity of cities[4] over many years. This has revealed hidden attributes that drive a city and determine its future, and these principally have psychological roots. This should not surprise us since cities are their people, the networks, the tribal allegiances and institutions they form.

Delhi: This neglected rag shrouds the building, but reveals the mindset of the city, which impacts on its people.

All these attributes have an impact on how the story of a city unfolds, how it makes the most of its resources and potentials, how it addresses setbacks and dramatic events and how its acts itself out in the world. The collective behaviour of the psyches of individuals and organisations when amalgamated and merged determine the spirit of the city, its atmosphere, its sense of soul.

Ghent, for instance, has a deep-seated attitude of self-criticism. This spurs the city to do better through its continual questioning even though it can come across as lacking in confidence. This fiercely independent city was often occupied by foreign troops so history played its part in its psychological response to circumstance.

A cliché about Adelaide in South Australia with a strong element of truth is that the city is intellectual and 'good at talking, less good at walking the walk'. This is not surprising since it was the only city in Australia created by idealistic free-settlers. That progressive foundation enabled it to create positive change, for example by being the first place to give women the full vote in 1894. It can be seen as a little high-minded, with a self-perception that Adelaide is better than all those other upstart cities that have sacrificed a good quality of life in order to chase gaudy ambitions.

Bilbao grapples with forceful natural elements, has a strong exploratory instinct, and a unique ethno-linguistic background. It was genetically isolated and has the highest proportion of the RH blood group in the world, yet was very influential in sailing exploration, its sailors reaching the icy shores of Northern Canada in the early 1500s, and the Basque explorer Elcano took over captaincy of Magellan's ship when he was killed to complete the first circumnavigation of the world. Castilian dominance has acted to torture its past and affected present ambitions for independence. This has reinforced the sense of pride in Basque identity and perhaps the city is too proud to be reflective.

Take New Yorkers, how they think of themselves and we think of them. The City's pressure cooker quality, in which it constantly needs to perform, generates ideas, projects and trade that etches itself into the psyche of the people as a 'can do' place, for better or worse. Big city people walk and eat faster, perhaps think faster, they say 10% more than townspeople. The media images of New York construct and reinforce these perceptions.

London has that odd mix of tradition, creativity and eccentricity where having ideas is easier than making them happen. It is a city whose history and language creates a vortex effect drawing in talent from everywhere. Perhaps this can make a city rest on its laurels.

Sydney is a place whose atmosphere is brash, determined and achievement-driven whereas, so the cliché goes, Melbourne seeks achievement at a more considered pace and is seen as more refined.

Trieste, feeling it is always stuck at the edge, was obstructed endlessly by Venetian sea power and then later embraced protection from the Habsburgs whose glittering sea port

*Corniglia: The urge to
be alone together*

it became. After World War I a victorious Italy moved into Trieste. The Slovene names were switched to Italian and then followed ongoing border disputes, forced Italianization, Nazi occupation, the decimation of the Jewish population and the formation of the only concentration camp on Italian soil. Today Trieste feels a little sad, like it is looking for a role and a less disturbed identity so it can face the future with clarity.

Mannheim in Germany, whose string of discoveries include Carl Benz's car. Seen as industrial and ugly, the core was destroyed in World War II and this external battering leads many Mannheimers to apologize too much. This shapes its self-image and can turn the city inwards. But in its undergrowth, it has one of the most vibrant German music scenes.

We think of Athens with the weight of its gloried past to which the present can never measure up, Beijing with its sense of being at the centre of the world, Tel Aviv as the first all-Jewish city in modern times which maintains it pioneering spirit and is now a global start-up hub, while Dubai's recent explosion onto the world stage is sharply shaping Dubaians' sense of self and destiny.

These city stories and their historic facts can have deep psychological effects, with the past reflected in the present, determining the future for a city as it can do for a person. They are therefore worthy of consideration.

27
IX
0016

SCHOOLS OF PSYCHOLOGY & THEIR URBAN POTENTIAL

There are several distinctly different branches of psychology. Here we summarise the main schools which can help urban thought and practice, each one providing insights.

In fact, implicit and under-acknowledged psychological thinking is present in many urban disciplines. Our aim is to make this far more explicit and to get city-makers to see its importance. Good urban design, for instance, asks itself how you create pleasing environments that encourage people and feel comfortable to interact. Planning guidelines seek to create the conditions for a better life based on thinking through the characteristics of what 'better' means. Mobility specialists increasingly understand that seamless connectivity is vital. Understanding the psychological drivers behind these desires will increase our ability to meet them.

Psychodynamic

Psychodynamic theory reviews how emotions, thoughts, early-life experiences and beliefs shape a person's present-day life and the coping mechanisms they have developed.

Disciplines commonly employing this approach include psychoanalysis and psychotherapy as well as counselling and general mental health practice. There is a proliferation of different schools which have moved on significantly from early thinkers like Adler, Jung, Freud and Klein. The theory of the unconscious is held in common, as is a set of principles about the dynamics of relationships and the importance of symbolism.

Ideas flowing from psychodynamics have been especially influential in the creative and artistic fields, yet remain virtually unexplored in relation to the city. One excellent example, however, is 'Psyche & the City' a collection of twenty inspiring essays and fiction[5] written by Jungian analysts about their cities and how a city's psyche can affect urban life. Psychodynamics can make a solid 'contribution to public policy as it provides an analysis of people's emotional experiences within social systems, not apart from them'[6].

Buenos Aires: Cities can delight with uplifting and surprising experiences.

Acknowledging the 'psyche of a city' and applying psychodynamics could radically shift our understanding of a place and its potential future. If, for instance, a city's lack of confidence is revealed and, since no 'urban confidence building' departments exist, a cross-disciplinary programme could be developed, generating experiences that lift the collective spirit, to trigger a sense of progress and belonging to a larger whole.

Behavioural

Used extensively in commercial marketing, behavioural psychology seeks to influence people's actions, feelings and thoughts, and is now almost commonly applied to social policy. It has been criticised for seeing drivers of behaviour change as entirely externally prompted, as if we have no free will, without considering its internal sources and was early on associated with social engineering.

Moving on from the ideas of its founders, particularly Watson and Skinner, behavioural interventions have proven highly successful. Behavioural Insights Ltd, nicknamed the 'Nudge Unit', originally a UK government initiative, has scored notable successes including the following.

• Ease of use: increasing payments through empirical research into what process people find easiest.

• Social norms: speeding up tax payments by telling people that most others pay their tax on time.

• Personalisation: Increasing the payment of fines by texting people 10 days before bailiffs were due.

• Incentives: providing lottery prizes to increase electoral participation rates.

The potential of behavioural psychology for cities is enormous and its influence will grow. It is important therefore to be aware that behaviourism applied in this way is not necessarily about helping people to better adapt in a permanent or embedded way to urban life, or enabling the city to meet psychological needs. Instead it seeks to administrate people towards specific behaviours, based on a judgement of what is 'good' and 'bad' behaviour. We have a responsibility to remain questioning about in whose service this powerful set of tools is[7], and to apply it ethically.

The potential for behavioural psychology is enormous ... we must apply it ethically

Taipei: Hidden unconscious depths can burst out through the city's seams, by British artist Filthy Luker in Very Fun Park 2013

Cognitive

Cognitive psychology helps people identify problems and formulate specific goals, tapping in to memory, language, perception and learning patterns. It is widely used in counselling, and is highly successful in tackling specific issues, for example phobias or non-clinical depression.

Cognitive approaches have been criticised for being overly mechanistic, for example seeing the brain as a computer. This view has been challenged by the idea of 'embodied cognition'[8] – that the mind and its processes are deeply affected by the body and not separate from it – stressing the importance of our relationship with the physical environment.

Gestalt psychology originated many of the principles of cognitive methods, demonstrating that the mind is constantly active and seeks meaning in the forms and experiences it encounters, but also that it can be fooled[9].

Gestalt theory has been successfully applied to visual design, using the 'laws' of similarity, symmetry, proximity, continuation[10] which have influenced urban design and architecture. The influential Commission for Architecture and the Built Environment, a UK government initiative, developed a striking evidence base of how different designs do and do not work well (hospitals, homes, schools, neighbourhoods). These approaches, combined with cognitive psychology, are a useful tool for assessing urban designs, asking what their emotional and psychological impacts would be.

Since cognitive theory tends to approach people more holistically than behavioural theory alone, it helps deliver insights into what makes us feel comfortable, at ease and fulfilled.

Humanistic

Humanistic psychology focuses on characteristics shared by all human beings such as love, grief, caring, and self-worth and the fulfilment of human potential. It considers earlier psychological schools as too narrow and too focused on what is wrong, illness rather than health. Maslow (and his now infamous 'Hierarchy') developed some of the central humanistic ideas about self-actualisation, an innate drive to reach human potential and the importance of internal-external perceptions such as self-esteem.

Other branches of psychology can view humanistic approaches as rather woolly, unscientific and linked to 'self-help' manuals. But their influence across other disciplines has been profound and lasting, but more focused on individuals rather than places[11]. There is however a clear link to concerns about well-being and happiness in cities and in considering the whole person. Humanistic psychology asks how essential human needs can be met, from basic safety to finding meaning, belonging and a sense of well-being.

Positive

There is now a shift to look at peoples' potential rather than weaknesses

Linked to humanists, positive psychologists[12] [13] argued, from the 1990s onward, that mainstream psychology mainly concerns itself with the shortcomings of individuals and their problems rather than their potential. It focused more on researching what makes life worth living. Humanists, like Maslow, Carl Rogers, and Eric Fromm helped renew interest in the more positive aspects of human nature. It has developed a broad, overarching framework associated with authors such as Martin Seligman and Mihaly Csikszentmihalyi.

It operates on three levels — the subjective, the individual and the group. The first explores positive experiences such as joy, well-being, satisfaction, contentment, happiness, optimism, flow and feeling good. The individual level looks at the personal qualities of a 'good life' and 'good person' emphasizing strengths such as courage, perseverance, forgiveness, originality, wisdom and interpersonal skills. The group level considers factors that foster citizenship and community-building including social responsibilities, altruism, civility or tolerance. It influenced the study of happiness and wellbeing now part of the urban policy repertoire, and as a field has massive potential for cities.

Archetypal

James Hillman, a Jungian psychologist and founder of archetypal psychology, set himself apart from the clinical psychiatric community, investigating the realm of imagination, enduring metaphors, myths and the deepest patterns of psychic functioning – "the fundamental fantasies that animate all life". In 'going deep' in this way, Hillman noted that imagination is more powerful than rational beliefs and continuously seeps through into consciousness, providing clues to the dynamics and organising principles of the psyche, where apparent chaos has an underlying order.

... there is a richer internal world full of images, metaphors, myths that our "I" inhabits.

He focused on the archai, the primary senses, the beginnings, the origins. In wishing to extend therapy beyond the medical world he aimed to care for the psyche and enable what he called 'soul making'. For Hillman 'soul' is more a perspective than a thing, a "dimension of experiencing life and ourselves," that allows the essence of what we are and could be to emerge in all its depth, in an integrated and genuine way, deriving its special register from knowledge of death. The essence of self in this view is not the isolated Cartesian "I think therefore I am" but a richer internal world full of images, metaphors, myths that this "I" inhabits.[14]

Archetypal psychology's goal is to draw out these potentials into the world via the creative acts of the individual, not to exclude them for the sake of social standards. Hillman, like Jung, believed it is folly to think human beings have transcended an archaic awareness of spirit inherent in the world.

As we set out in Chapter 7 (Soul and the City), archetypal psychology's potential for the city is in recapturing a kind of animism for the modern world, seeing cities as living organisms not machines, inseparable from their makers, and which embody

their thoughts. This chimes well with more recent theories of physics and appears to up-end the current Western, scientific view that the world is knowable, and mechanistically reducible to its component parts. Yet archetypal psychology can be seen as adding to that view because it deals with the messy complexity of issues which bubble up regardless: a search for meaning, religious concerns, fear of mortality, the imagination and creativity, and it sees the city as the amphitheatre in which these can co-exist.

Evolutionary

Evolutionary psychology explores why and how humans act the way they do over time in adapting to changing environments and challenges. It brings together evolutionary biology with cognitive psychology, linked to anthropology and is potentially highly relevant to an urban psychology.

For example, stereotyping is a behaviour which may have evolutionary origins, as it can have survival value as a mental strategy in high risk situations (and is often associated with people in high risk professions and institutions), but ultimately leads to conflict in the urban arena.

Bari: Even the dull, done well, can be quite attractive.

Evolutionary psychology often takes a Darwinian approach which can seem rather cold[16], and, with its links to cognitive psychology, it tends to view the mind as an 'organic computer', with modules developed within it – for example, for the compelling notion of an innate linguistic capacity. Some have criticised it , perhaps unfairly, for being overly reductive, and touching on eugenics, with an unhealthy relationship to racial psychology. Instead of seeing the human mind as rigid and fixed by its development in the African Savannah, it posits that it emerges from a collective set of evolutionary 'guidelines' and flexible resources that can be deployed to suit different circumstances and over which we have some control. Greater knowledge of these forces can help us understand how the dramatic impacts of the digitized world are shaping peoples' mindscape as it links and adapts to deep-rooted evolutionary needs with the blending of virtual and real worlds and especially developments in artificial intelligence.

Social and cultural

Social psychology studies how people act, think, and feel in the context of society and how these things change as we interact with others. Cultural psychology looks at how behavioural patterns are rooted and embodied in culture whereas psychological anthropology studies the interaction of cultural and mental processes. Especially it explores 'enculturation', the process by which people learn the requirements of their surrounding culture and acquire appropriate values and behaviours. The history, language, practices, and conceptual landscape of a person or a place shape human understanding, emotion, perception, motivation and mental health.

... social and cultural differences and similarities, personality types or group thinking influence behaviour

The relevance to cities is strong with its emphasis on interpersonal relationships, understanding social and cultural differences and similarities, personality types, group behaviour, and how these influence behavioural development and learning, particularly of children.

Crucial to cities, politics and leadership the (in)famous 'Milgram Experiment'[17] of the 1950's showed how group pressure can lead to people agreeing with clearly false statements so as to conform. Here participants were convinced by an authority figure in a white coat with clipboard to administer increasingly large electric shocks to levels they were aware could be fatal, to someone they

could not see but could hear screaming – and even dying – behind a screen as the shocks were applied. The screams came from an actor.

Milgram went on to explicitly study urban psychology and published influential ideas about how to explore urban-emotional impacts[18] which we would do well to revisit.

Conflict resolution negotiations between divided communities can often focus on issues of land, money and power, neglecting the basic building blocks of interpersonal relationships. The 'peace psychologists' Herbert Kelman and John Burton, whose work is increasingly important given urban tensions, adapted the work of Maslow[19], showing how basic psychological needs had to be met before progress on negotiations could be made. They include: feeling secure; belonging; self-esteem and respect; a right to cultural identity; an ability to participate; and a sense of fairness – sometimes, a simple apology.

Studies suggest many of these needs are innate, or at the least appear extremely early in our development, which raises a central question for any city or indeed neighbourhood: to what extent is this place meeting (or getting in the way of) our basic psychological needs especially in the context of rising populism? The answer may fundamentally determine the success of a place and the ability of communities to co exist.

Another example is the evidence that levels of day to day social contact and interaction between people in neighbourhoods – virtually and physically – correlates directly to levels of trust and cohesion[20].

The enormous potential in applying these areas of psychology to cities is obvious given the challenges of groups with different outlooks living in close proximity. Understanding how social networks operate and what our fundamental needs are provide clear lessons for successful place making.

day to day social contact … correlates directly to levels of trust

Neuroscience

The advances in neuroscience are so transformational to our understanding of planning that it may become a central feature of future urban practice. The field is growing and fashionable, investigating the human brain, from the functional organisation

*Genova: Graffiti can express
our aspiration, for a drink or
something more.*

of large scale cerebral systems to microscopic neurochemical processes. Technological advances have allowed scientists to directly observe the brain in action, for example when making decisions, experiencing emotion and having new ideas or employing creative thinking. The findings of neuroscience are entirely evidence based, and open a window into many questions of psychology that were previously only theoretical.

Yet the implications from this work are more speculative and often controversial, for example questioning free will (as brain activity can be apparent before a conscious decision to act is registered), or suggesting that computers will be able to replicate brain functioning and even consciousness (an idea hotly rejected by some neuroscientists[21]), straying into philosophy and spawning the field of 'neuroethics'.

the findings of neuroscience are evidence based ... its implications more speculative and controversial

Despite the claims of neuroscience, this does not mean it alone will explain everything psychology has been grappling with, or supplant its existing insights. Emotions like anger, love and compassion, and functions like creativity have all been associated with chemicals and regions in the brain; they have been 'located' biologically.

But these triggers have a source linking complex interactions of internal and external stimuli, associations and other factors which trigger brain activity, influenced by our childhood, culture, environment and genes. The brain is not separate from the world, or indeed the rest of the body, as argued in respect of embodied cognition. Knowing how or where a process happens is not the same as understanding what it means and where it comes from.

The advances in neuroscience are however game changing and their potential applications to urban living profound. We can now wear headsets of neuro-transmitters that will record brain activity as we walk around a city, giving another layer of definition and vast data sources to work with[22].

Environmental

... where we live influences our sense of self, and is instrumental in fostering belonging

Environmental psychology explores interactions between differing physical environments and human behaviour and perception, including the built and the natural. It has focused on cities, urban design and architecture and is intimately connected with the sustainability agenda. This field assesses, for instance, how physical environments feel for citizens, such as the draining dullness of blank walls, jarring juxtapositions of buildings and how some feel cold, external or monotonous. It looks at how high-rise blocks can make people feel diminished as overwhelming structures can diminish a person's sense of self or control so engendering fear and how, by contrast, the effects of soft light are welcoming.

Two influential concepts of environmental psychology are 'place identity' and 'place attachment', developed by Proshansky, Schroeder and others in the 1960s-80s. Place identity explores how where we live – and particularly where we grow up – influences our sense of self, and is instrumental in fostering belonging, purpose and meaning in one's life (or lack of it). Place here refers also to community, and the shared sense of a city's wider identity, as well as that of individual neighbourhoods. The positive or negative returns from place identity are based on the extent to which a place meets people's psychological, social and cultural needs, and can have long term emotional impacts for individuals. Place attachment looks more specifically at emotional attachments to a place, and suggests that both the amount and quality of time spent in a place are key determinants in that relationship. Attachment can fracture when the new norm is nomadic; there is mobility and not only for people, but for capital, for jobs, for commodities, for information, for ideas. Environmental psychology is ahead of the pack in applying research to urban settings and has its professional associations and well-developed conference programmes.

Psychogeography

This is not a branch of psychology, but a unique and distinctive way of exploring and representing the city with much to offer. Originating in the French Avant-garde and Lettrist movements, calling on Baudelaire's notion of the 'Flaneur', a 'casual urban wanderer[23]', it combines highly original and playful views of the city with different art forms, particularly creative writing, to reinterpret the city and how it is experienced, unlocking new ideas.

The works of the French Situationist International or Peter Ackroyd's books on London are examples, as are Will Self's and Ralph Steadman's regular articles on psychogeography.[24] They provide a different route to engaging with a place, cutting through statistics, plans and strategies to get at feeling, intuition and meaning. Psychogeography is reminiscent of the way in which psychodynamic theory attempts to understand our relationship to place, and points toward the value of mixing artistic with psychological approaches to cities.

... it engages with place differently, cutting through statistics, and plans to get at feeling, intuition and meaning.

Mixing the thinking

Psychology effortlessly spans the divides between science, philosophy and belief. This has brought elements of some psychologies into conflict with more purist rationalist perspectives since concepts such as the individual or collective unconscious, even the idea of 'mind', are difficult to prove in any objective sense. Yet, it is often in the gaps between disciplines or at their margins where different perspectives rub up against each other that the most imaginative ideas or solutions emerge.

To fully understand the psychological complexities of a person, organisation or especially a city, multiple perspectives are needed rather than a single glorious truth. Ideas which appear opposing to those who drew the battle lines (and stand to lose or gain) can coexist peacefully and cross-fertilise new thinking within urban policy.

An example is to bring the insights of two of the great ways of knowing – materialism and idealism – together. Materialism – a perspective requiring physical evidence – and idealism – one that does not – are frequently pitted against each other as opposites and this can impoverish debate and solutions. Materialism and idealism can be of mutual benefit, either in generating creative thinking or by extending possibilities through new evidence and discovery.

"The opposite of a fact is a falsehood, but the opposite of a profound truth may be another profound truth."

The Danish Physicist Niels Bohr noted aptly: "The opposite of a fact is a falsehood, but the opposite of one profound truth may very well be another profound truth." He acknowledges that a materialist scientific perspective fails to explain away concepts like personal narrative, the desire for completion or meaning, which are essential to human endeavour and wellbeing, and so also to cities

Another necessary blending is with the smart cities agenda. This harnesses the potential of vast big data sets with self-regulating, responsive sensors and is having a transformative impact on places. There has been a strong re-orientation from its corporate origins. Eurocities, for instance, with its 130 members across 35 countries notes: 'There can be no smart city without smart citizens. Smarter cities are inclusive places that use technology and innovation to empower, engage with and capitalise on citizen participation. Engaging citizens goes beyond the uptake of technology; it extends to the co-creation of ideas and solutions'[25].

Here intellectual capacity and human emotional intelligence, instincts and feelings can be brought together to understand and solve what really matters. This is part of humanising urban policy and strategy by giving the emotional impact of decisions more equal weighting, and by gathering and understanding data from an emotional perspective.

The famous dumpling house Din Tai Fung reminds us of our sometimes robotic existence

Recent progress

In 2005 Harold Takooshian wrote a comprehensive summary of the state of urban psychology, coining the phrase 'Homo Urbanis'[26]. Perhaps his most important point is that, despite our planet urbanising at a staggering rate, only 4% of people in total human history have lived in cities. Yet the systematic study of urban psychology has gradually decreased since the 1970s. Ignorant of the above potential, we appear to have gone backwards, not forwards. There are of course exceptions.

The Biennial Conference of Environmental Psychology[27] is an important platform for extending the value that this area of study has already brought to cities. The 11th conference in Groningen, 2015 set out the following research agenda.

• How do the physical and social environments affect wellbeing and behaviour?

• Which environmental changes can enhance health and wellbeing?

• Which factors affect pro-environmental behaviour?

• Which strategies are effective and acceptable to encourage pro-environmental behaviour?

The Task Force on Urban Psychology, run by the American Psychological Association in New York in 2005, represented a major step forward, underlining how psychology can help improve urban living and "balances the all too frequent identification of urban life with deficits and pathology by giving attention to the strengths found in urban settings and among urban residents."[28]

The Task Force Report focused more on tackling issues like segregation, poverty and mental health through largely health-based intervention (which was its stated purpose), rather than aiming for a general urban policy shift towards being more psychologically aware. It does however set out a radical and innovative research agenda which national and international agencies should urgently consider.

A relatively new range of wellbeing and happiness indicators have evolved to reveal how different places impact on people emotionally (see Place, Purpose and Wellbeing below). Happiness trends can now be followed live, as they are in the Hedometer project[29], analysing key words on Twitter and the LondonMood project.

A raft of new measures are being developed to assess our state of mind

There is a growing trend for action research projects in cities to test their 'character', like The Lost Wallet Test[30] which left wallets full of cash on the streets of 16 well known global cities to see how many were handed in. Helsinki came out top with nearly all handed in, Lisbon did worst with only one handed in (by a couple on holiday from The Netherlands), and London came ninth with just less than half handed in.

One study concluded that cities that are in decline and feel unhappy now were also unhappy in their prosperous past[31], while another[32] explored the way in which the origins and histories of cities can shape their destinies.

The City Personality Test chapter describes work we have developed with eleven cities that seeks to draw on the lessons of this collective psychological work. Its aim is to start a practical, yet strategic conversation in cities about their urban psyche and what this could do for them.

Do our cities have a more male or female personality.

Preliminary conclusions

Even a cursory review of psychology reveals a deep reservoir of value for cities which is virtually untapped. No single model of psychology can claim to offer a complete understanding of the human-urban interface and how to positively develop it. And why should it. Rather, an approach utilising 'all the insights' will provide the best toolkit.

The current rate of urbanisation makes the need for greater understanding of urban psychology urgent, yet research and teaching in relation to this field has declined steadily since the 1970's. Despite this decline, the use of wellbeing indicators has increased, alongside an understanding of their economic importance, providing a platform for more detailed psychological studies, although as we go on to discuss, these are currently very limited and few operate at the level of the city.

... there is a deep reservoir of psychological insight untapped by cities

Instead of a rigid mental apparatus fixed at a specific moment in our evolution, we each own a set of flexible psychological resources capable of adapting well to cities, but this does not mean we are fully equipped for urban life. Our resources, resilience and physical and mental health can be restricted or enlarged by where and how we live and the physical and atmospheric conditions we create.

Cities are not in any inherent sense 'bad' for us, the benefits outweigh the negatives, socially, economically, culturally and environmentally. But we currently only have a faint grasp of the interdependencies between our cities and our sense of wellbeing, and the psychological impacts of urban planners, engineers, architects, urban designers and cultural activists. To create satisfying cities requires each to stretch beyond their subject knowledge, applying emotional intelligence.

... if we do not consider human psychological needs, serious negative consequences can follow

If our environment does not support common and basic human psychological needs and insights it can lead to serious personal, social and therefore economic dysfunction. Addressing these issues is complex in cities and the proper application of psychology will help. The potential utility of urban psychology is therefore threefold.

1. Facilitating a different way of looking at and connecting with the city, the psychological lens, that can unlock new perceptions, solutions and routes of exploration for residents and policy makers. The City Personality Test is an example of this.

2. Providing a new and complimentary toolkit for use alongside more conventional approaches, and which we begin to sketch out below. This could be deployed to support how we develop and plan cities, in terms of its urban form and functions, and for well-being, social and economic policies for success, measuring these as they are implemented.

3. Creating a set of tailored interventions to help city life and residents through research which applies psychological models to specific urban issues. This could impact significantly and positively on people and places.

Corniglia: someone considering our preliminary conclusions.

HOMO URBANIS & THE ARCHAIC MIND

Modern humans have been around for 200,000 years, but cities for only 6,000 to 8,000 years.

Of the estimated 107 billion[33] of us that have ever existed, hardly anyone has visited, never mind lived in a city. Yet cities have risen on a spectacular arc brick by mudbrick from the banks of the Euphrates to today's high-tech mega cities with populations the size of nations.

By 2050 70% of people will live in cities and in 2008[34] half the world's urban population surpassed the magic 50%. A hundred years ago it was only 20%, and exponentially less the further back in time we go. This trajectory has no parallels in history. So, if Bronowski's Ascent of Man had a sequel, it would be an urban edition.

We are a very – perhaps the most – adaptive species, but also unique in that we did not evolve in what is now our primary habitat. While colonising the globe, each change of environment, temperature and landscape resulted in changes in us, physically, psychologically, and culturally; but these changes have limits. Our bodies, for example, are still essentially stone age, so we struggle to cope with modern foods, sugars and processed fats.

Just as the body is the museum of human evolution so the psyche is the mental museum of our primeval psychological past, and we have carried anciently formed elements of it into this new urban age. Important clues to a better urban future could be revealed by asking if the same holds true of the relationship between our mind and our cities.

Long-standing behaviours shaping humanity over the millennia shifted quickly to enable us to live in cities, with psychological consequences. Some studies show a link between urban living conditions and poorer mental health, with urban populations twice as likely to experience schizophrenia, and almost three times as likely to experience depression than those in rural areas[35]. These figures highlight that poverty, the biggest single indicator of ill health, is concentrated in cities. But cities are

Lisbon: What city walls keep in - and condense - is as important as what they keep out.

also capable of building positive mental health and psychological robustness: they ask us to live in diverse conditions, respect others views, and cope with clamour and change.

The Triune Brain Theory[36] suggests that our brains carry ancient components from well before the African Savannah. The reptilian part of our brain evolved first and is responsible for basic, instinctive functions, aggression, fight or flight. The ancient mammalian part of the brain is built upon it, responsible for more complex functions like motivation, emotion and parenting. The most recent part of the brain, the neocortex, deals with higher functions like planning, abstract thinking and language. The newer, higher functions can be overruled by the older, even when the conscious 'I' does not want that to happen. We lose our temper inappropriately or freeze in the face of challenges we know we can master, reptilian responses to perceived threats.

Beijing: Is this how we want to live.

Portland: Understanding the need for nature and for spaces to reflect.

This is an oversimplification, but it highlights how our evolutionary past is deeply embedded in our present. It can influence our responses and reactions, how we feel and behave in ways we have limited control over. We might therefore better understand our new urban mindscape by looking for traces of our past within it. Two examples we include below are the effects of the unprecedented scale and density of urban populations, and increased calls on our time and our attention. In the subsequent chapter, we go on to look at our psychological relationship to our physical surroundings.

Mind of a Village, Body of a City

The village preceded the city and remains nostalgically in the affections of city dwellers from London to Tokyo, Moscow to New York. Evolutionary anthropology suggests this is partly because it can be challenging for us to relate meaningfully to more than 150 people at a time (the 'Dunbar Number'[37], although other anthropologists put this figure nearer 250). This was probably the average number in hunter-gather tribes, and was around the average population in villages right up until the 18th Century.

Film, TV and literature often represent the village as an idyllic location, sending rural characters into cities to make the point, from David Copperfield to Crocodile Dundee. Yet in reality this Arcadian past never existed. Historically, rural life was for most one of grinding poverty and the seat of unrest until recent times.

There is an assumption too that villages work well because everyone knows each other, and cities should replicate this. While a sense of community is fundamental to being human, the city allows for a refreshing feeling of anonymity, an escape from behaviour dictated by the village elders, and gives the ability to choose an alternative social group and reinvent oneself. Crowds can be soothing and provide fascination, the people-watching we find so irresistible outside a café, pub or public square increases our sense of interest, wellbeing and security. The restrictions of a too-close community can positively give way to neighbourly civility in cities, where a simple greeting is enough to maintain the contact we want, and instead of being scrutinised we might be more respectfully and mutually observed, feeling we are of some interest to others and that their help would be available if needed.

Since cities are so new, one could say we are living with the mind of a village in the body of a city. Cities that work well know almost instinctively how to organise themselves around the positive aspects of close-knit communities.

Crowds in cities can be soothing and the intimacy of villages can close us in

This has been recognised from model villages to Ebenezer Howard's Town and Country Planning and more recent Urban Village movements. Each makes a contribution, but cities should avoid producing a parody of the medieval village.

The strength and innate resources of urban neighbourhoods demonstrate the positive dynamics that emerge in response to urban life and how cities can help people thrive. Yet it can be challenging to maintain a sense of the collective or responsible and engaged citizenship across something as complex as a city with its amalgam of perspectives and cultures. Here psychology can offer insight.

Cities have allowed us to exceed our biological and intellectual limits, they are part of our evolution and not just as a technological innovation. No complex animal has ever lived together in such numbers and cities greatly intensify human networks and interactions and are capable of generating new thinking, amplifying creativity, passing it on and becoming a pressure cooker for ingenuity in ways villages never could.

Eco Systems and Ego Systems

The evident physical and social forms of cities make it easy to forget that the ego and the unconscious are also at play. Cities can intensify and concentrate the positive, but also the negative, like crime and poverty. It is important to acknowledge and face the complex and darker aspects, as within ourselves. When this is denied, the city and our relationship to it becomes fractured. We dissociate from it and project our un-owned fears upon the city and this can burst out in unsettling ways.

Cohesion and bonding are deep human traits that have immense survival value and are at the core of our social behaviours, which are still essentially tribal. We are hard-wired to bond and this allows us to feel what others feel and we may even derive our sense of self from interiorising our sense of community[38]. This has strong implications for urban policy. If our sense of community is weak, it will be difficult for us to work out who we are, or how we can relate well to each other. By understanding how to engender a stronger sense of empathy we can build a more robust and coherent civil society and stronger communities[39].

Empathy and tribal behaviour have a troubling side though. An American study[40] demonstrated that there has been a rise of special and minority interest groups since the 1970s. These have become more and more insular with members increasingly less-likely to meet people with different views, so leading to 'parallel lives', a concept first coined by Ted Cantle in 2004[41] and reinforced by the Casey Review surveys in Britain in 2016[42]. When people are surrounded only by those who agree with them, their views become more extreme, rigid and prejudiced. This dynamic is compounded by the limited number of close connections our brains are able to make, and once that limit is reached stereotyping, over-simplification and 'group-think' come into play.

A group mentality is great when something needs to get done without too many questions being asked, but less so when dealing with complexity and diversity, the day to day reality of urban life. This is one reason why rural dwellers tend to have far more conservative views of life than urbanites. They are simply not challenged by difference in the same way as their urban cousins.

Strengthening a bond with one group can therefore lead to flatly rejecting another, even to the point of seeing them as inhuman. In analytical psychology, this is called 'Othering' – labelling people in different social or gender groups as inferior – or the projection of the Shadow-Self[43], an attempt to deny or banish our own undesirable traits by projecting them onto another person or group, and then vilifying and rejecting them.

Yet today even tribalism is challenged, as the combination of consumer culture and urban living has fostered a culture of individualism with a reduced reliance on – or trust of – the collective. New technology may reshape that landscape.

Social media can polarise and even help radicalise, but also bring differing groups together in powerful ways. The LondonMood Project app as an example records how people feel several times a day in different environments[44] revealing the city's collective mood at any given moment. The emerging sharing economy of Airbnb, Uber and Freecycle is fundamentally reframing our sense of material ownership that might help counteract tribal tendencies and help us shift to being more engaged with others – from the sharing economy to the sharing society. So the city begins to address some of the biggest psychological questions facing humanity.

The energy of cities is derived from its varied identities, which can be marshalled as a collective spirit and force for good, where difference is valued. The many 'I 'Heart' My City' programmes are one testimony. One brought people onto the streets to clean up in Britain's cities after the riots of 2011. Another is the 'We love Helsinki' programme that encourages people to dance together. In these ways cities can become engines for empathy, and urban leadership can lead the way by showing a sense of civic generosity in tone and action.

Cities are places where the stranger and difference meet the tribal instinct and the basic human desire to connect. This dynamic drove the development of the concept of citizenship in Athens in 600BC and the obligations it entailed, and its later iteration in Rome, where the concept of legal citizenship emerged and since then has broadened to become ever more inclusive. Differing views of life and value-sets are a main cause of stress between urban neighbours. Creating zones of encounter with opportunities to mix and communicate can reduce tensions, emphasising what we share as human beings with the same basic psychology more than what separates us, and building social capital. Understanding these dynamics can support the reinvention of citizenship for the modern context.

In cities the desire to connect with difference meets with the tribal instinct to be separate

Anyone concerned with development and innovation, from business to universities and beyond, understands the need for

Venice: Imagine what it would be like if things were reversed. Artwork by AES+F the Russian collective.

exposure to difference in order to force-feed new thinking and solutions. Consider how numerous places across the world from MIT Rad Lab in Boston, Aalto University in Helsinki, Berlin's programme to fund interdisciplinary institutions to the new Crick Institute in Britain operate. They build structures and management processes designed to foster interaction between different disciplines. An urban example is The Intercultural City Programme with now over 100 members, developed originally by Comedia and now managed by the Council of Europe. This provides advice, methods and evaluation processes to help cities develop in an intercultural way.

The Bauhaus School founded by Walter Gropius in Weimar and later based in Dessau was a mighty inter-disciplinary force which still echoes today. Its spirit could be reinvented in the present. In the same way that Bauhaus mixed up disciplines to revolutionise the design of individual objects and buildings, what we need now is a 'Bauhaus for Place', looking at the complexity of the whole

... workplaces that bring together differing insights are mostly more successful

Jantar Mantar in Delhi the astonishing complex of buildings from 1724 that measured astronomic tables.

built and socio-economic urban landscape, with psychologists, economists, sociologists, anthropologists, as well as designers, artists and planners involved.

Time's Arrow and Boomerang Minds

... demands on attention are proliferating and causing mental overload

We see time in cities as a universal constant, 'the march of time' or 'the arrow of time' relentlessly proceeding in a single direction, that we must use or lose. Time is speeded up in cities – the urban accelerator effect – so frenetically we try to cram it all in, or maybe are frozen with indecision in the headlights of a hopeless number of choices.

Demands on attention proliferate, from video screen advertising to piped muzak creating cognitive overload as our minds boomerang back and forth between competing messages. This fragments and diverts us away from an internally driven pattern of thought towards one driven by external distractions. Yet our sense of self is built on an internal narrative which begins at an extremely early age, continues throughout life[45] and requires space and peace, something recognised in schools' Quiet Zones. The stories we tell ourselves are a big part of how we become us, and they require calm and reflective time to develop. No wonder mindfulness is all the rage or the new 'digital detox movement' has emerged. Calmness is increasingly hard to find in cities.

Cities are increasingly following the lead of schools and some offices, creating protective spaces where calm reflection is possible. São Paolo, then Chennai and later Grenoble and Tehran, concerned with visual pollution, took the lead in banning billboards. Another response is the Slow Cities Movement in Italy Cittaslow growing out of the Slow Food Movement, with 143 members in 24 countries, based on taking time to appreciate the finer qualities of place. Slow not fast food, locally produced, where you could identify the maker. The movement encourages people to meander like Baudelaire's Flaneur[46], a hunter-gatherer of urban experiences, not always to be the rushing commuter. Its members tend to be places that are also environmentally forward looking.

Time is a constant for physicists, but for human perception it is a construct. Concepts of time between modern cultures can be very different. The Mediterranean view of time is not the same as that of the more punctual Northern Europeans, and in the East is seen as more cyclical than linear. In Japan time unfolds in a ritual fashion and in Buddhist Thailand is fluid and less permanent.[47][48]

In ancient cultures time was perceived differently again. The North America Hopi tribe have no word for time, the Amazonian Piraha people have no past tense or word for future and live constantly in the present. Nomadic peoples tend to see time only as a seasonal cycle.

The human mind has historically experienced time in a more organic or cyclical way, and even a shared measurement of time is relatively recent, arriving with the dawn of rail travel. How we construct and use our time defines the texture and quality of our existence, and is central to our perceptual landscape.

Organic time might be described as living in the continuous moment. The present is fluid, infinite, expanded. Our most ancient ancestors probably experienced time in this way, not always for positive reasons. Surviving in the early stone age would tend to focus one's mind on the here and now.

Cyclical time is a rhythmic experience, linked to seasonal change which would have had a profound meaning for both hunter gatherers and early farmers. Agricultural societies often

... the perception of rhythmic, cyclical and linear time are different in cities

expressed this perception of birth, growth, decay, death and rebirth in their mythology. The rhythms of cyclical time create a sense of regularity and predictability, so that if things are bad the wheel can turn to the good. There is a sense of an endless, unlimited supply of time.

Linear time took over after the industrial revolution, as people became distant from a deep sense of seasonal change and the clock began to rule daily life. There was rhythm, but grey, unvarying. Time in this perception is a commodity – it literally is money – and benefits and negatives follow. A strongly linear perception of time is associated with anxiety and depression as everything races ahead and people cannot see an end point, they are neither in the moment nor do they have the certainty that the moment will change. Shifting that perception can relieve such symptoms.

Both cyclical and organic time are more immersive and have a sense of being impersonal, all-embracing. Time is not just something that happens to us as individuals, but it happens to communities and the world around us, which made people feel they were part of a bigger whole. Linear time feels more personal and less communal, and this perception of time is linked to shifts in views on, and fears of, mortality. In cyclical time the tribe, the people and the place go on. In personal irreversible linear time, death is the end point.

Urban time tends to pass in this linear way and is connected to the notion of the city as a clockwork-driven machine. Linear time can feel like a straight-jacket, so deeper desires burst out through its seams into cultural activity, festivals and celebration. This suggests a yearning for a partial return to more rhythmic or organic cycles or the ability to lose oneself in the moment as demonstrated in: the Winter Festival of Light in Helsinki; Fasching in Germany; Rio's Carnival; La Tomatina and the many food and fertility festivals in Spring and Summer; and the proliferation of music and alternative life-style festivals globally.

the experience of the city as a clockwork driven machine can feel constraining

Culture and cultural activity derive from fundamental human needs and help us to define the relationship between ourselves and others, the world, its things and places. Culture proceeds from our psychology and is a means both of investigating and amplifying these relationships. Cities that take culture seriously

Delhi: Chaotic yet organic at the same. time, yet is it too much.

tend to do better than those that do not, as do those that embrace openness, tolerance and diversity[49].

Cities are very recent in evolutionary terms and although humans are adaptive this new urban habitat can have negative psychological impacts. We can thrive in cities and they can bring out the best in us if we understand the misalignment between our archaic and modern senses of self, and how that may cause psychological dis-ease, disturbance and illness. The lessons from our lived primitive experience are that we need rhythm, cycle, as well as places and events to step out of time, to lose or find ourselves, and quiet space to reflect on who we are and might become. This helps build aspiration, purpose and a sense of meaning.

Psychology holds some answers and ideas to help us adapt as we shift from Homo Sapiens to Homo Urbanis. The cities that will do best may well be those most able to bring our ancient and modern parts together.

Humans are adaptive, but the dramatic rise of cities challenges our psychological apparatus

PLACE, PURPOSE AND WELLBEING

Examining our psychological roots suggests that there is an innate human drive toward life satisfaction, fulfilment and wholeness, but that this process is not guaranteed.

City-making strategies and the resulting local quality of life can help or hinder. The emerging science of happiness and wellbeing tries to measure aspects of this, increasingly considered an indicator of socio-economic progress and a goal of public policy, from the Happy Planet Index to the World Happiness report[50]. The UK Office for National Statistics surveys wellbeing regionally, but it does not tell us much about cities other than London. Other surveys tend to be national or regional at best, and should also be conducted at city-level, not in order to create a blunt league table, but to tell us more about local strengths and weaknesses and how they can be addressed.

But is 'happy' the right measure at all? It is mostly used to describe this or that life satisfaction which gives pleasure, contentment or joy. Yet the terms of happiness can change with fashion, as a temporary sensation of feeling good rather than a deeper sense of fulfilment rooted in meaning and purpose. Happiness can be an awkward, uncomfortable word. It can be self-referential and with a strong ring of entitlement. It seems to demand from others, having an expectation that someone else should make us happy, at work, in a relationship, in a city. To chase happiness directly can be elusive, as Nathaniel Hawthorne notes: "Happiness is a butterfly, which when pursued, is always just beyond your grasp, but which, if you will sit down quietly, may alight upon you".

Urban psychology points toward a more profound aim: to create the fundamental conditions which avoid misery and provide an environment that might then let happiness emerge as a consequence of increased wellbeing, which is defined as contentment, welfare and dignity. Happiness and wellbeing are often used interchangeably and Stuart McReady's survey of happiness across the millennia, the continents and cultures unscrambles well the ideas and ideals[51].

Manila: The external manifestations of meaning change over time, but the basic human need for meaning persists.

Happiness is only one part of wellbeing and not the same as fulfilment based on meaning and purpose. There has been much more research on the former rather than the latter, although Roy Baumeister[52] has researched this and concluded: "Satisfying one's needs and wants increased happiness but was largely irrelevant to meaningfulness. Happiness was largely present-oriented, whereas meaningfulness involves integrating past, present, and future" Reinforcing the entitlement point above, happiness was linked to being more a receiver than a giver, but – to back up the old adage – to create meaningfulness, giving was more important than receiving.

This study also showed that concerns with personal identity and self-expression contribute to a sense of purpose in life because 'happiness without meaning characterizes a relatively shallow, self-absorbed or even selfish life, in which things go well, needs and desires are easily satisfied, and difficult or taxing entanglements are avoided'. This does not describe a resilient or mature person (or place), yet there are massive cultural pressures to be happy and in a three-month period in early 2013 about 1,000 books on happiness appeared on Amazon even though 'meaning is healthier than happiness'.[53]

In cities, happiness can be strongly associated with consuming and with a social status defined by what we can or cannot afford, the 'intricacies of urban hierarchies' revealed[54] by purchases, not just jobs. An endless loop of over-consumption does not bring happiness, but having money matters up to a point. Beyond a certain level other needs and wishes come to the fore.[55][56]

The strong correlation in wellbeing indices between unhappiness and economically unequal places is no surprise. Persistently low living standards have a pernicious effect, as studies like the Royal Society of Arts Inclusive Growth Commission[57], and the PWC Good Growth Index confirm.

American researcher Patricia Greenfield has unearthed a direct correlation between urbanization in the US and a move toward more materialistic language, over a 200-year period. Using software, her analysis of 1.2 million books published between 1800 and 2000 suggested a fundamental shift away from a deference to authority and a collaborative way of thinking, to one that is more individualistic and materialistic, from an interdependent way of being to one of a "crowd of individuals". These changes map precisely to rising levels of urbanization. But other factors like the rise of enlightenment ideas are also significant.

Daily urban challenges like commuting can have a decisive impact on happiness. Someone with a one-hour commute has to earn 40 percent more to be as satisfied as someone who walks to work, and swapping a long commute for a walk to work creates the same happiness level as forming a new romantic attachment[58]. Other impacts include crowded living conditions and low levels of social interaction within communities, whether people do or do not feel included, validated and listened to in the plans of city-makers.

Sao Paolo: What feelings does this combination of buildings engender.

A review by the New Economics Foundation[59] of the evidence for wellbeing, beyond the basics of not living in poverty, having a job, resources or housing, summaries this well. They suggest five actions for day-to-day life. Connect: with family, friends, colleagues and neighbours at home, work, school or in the local community. Think of these as cornerstones of life and invest time in developing them. Be active: walk, run, cycle, play, garden, dance. Be curious: notice, be aware, feel, catch the different and unusual, ask why and reflect. Learn: explore something new, rediscover old interests, take on different responsibilities, fix things, play, cook, learn to play an instrument, set a challenge. Give: do something for someone without wanting a return favour, thank someone, smile, volunteer, see oneself linked to a wider community.

In happiness surveys, it is not always obvious why some places score highly, and it can be difficult to work out the difference between how people feel because of where they live, or because of other internal or relationship factors (such as deciding on a scale of responses from 'I cry a lot' to 'My life has meaning').

Cities can be the solution not the problem, but as society urbanizes there are distinct impacts arising from city living. Happiness analysis builds on psychological methods, but we should go much further by creating more radical models of investigation of deeper urban wellbeing. New tools are also needed to detect the subtle and lumbering undercurrents of social change from urban living, the effects of which can be profound. The purpose of these tools should be to help cities ask important questions about how they can better meet the basic requirements of human wellbeing, rooted in an evidence based, psychological understanding of what those needs actually are.

Psychology by Design

Into our cities, we bring environmental connections from our elemental past, potentially directly affecting our sense of wholeness and wellbeing. Bonding to nature and greenery is one of the most ancient. Seeing greenery – even photographs of it – can calm people and lower blood pressure. Hospital wards that look out onto greenery have faster patient recovery times, and being near water has similar results, as the pioneering work of Roger Ulrich from the late 1980's onwards and other research has shown[60]. This is reflected too in higher property values near natural assets.[61]

Green space impacts positively on our psyche, as regularly experiencing a beautiful natural setting, particularly one that inspires a sense of awe and wonder, makes people more prosocial[62]: more agreeable, displaying empathy, trust and generosity. Access to parks can improve mental health, but the specific design features of the park are important. Quality matters – not just the quantity of urban greenery.

Our pattern of navigation of streets and urban spaces may also have an instinctive basis to it, perhaps developed in pre-urban environments in a way that still drives moment-to-moment choices. For example, Space Syntax[63] spun out of University College London, whose work supports the development of a psychological lens on the city, coined the term 'least angled space' to describe the way in which people intuitively take as few as possible turns and corners when walking from one point to another in a city, an idea reinforced by the 'desire lines' etched into parks that endlessly subvert attempts to route people over less direct – or less desirable – paved routes. Understanding these deep drivers of personal mobility will enable more informed design choices about how we can help people move with ease, and encourage different encounters as they do so.

Urban design has quite well understood effects on physical health[64] but also on mental health,[65] as the 'sanity and urbanity' blog of the Centre for Urban Design and Public Health encapsulates. Positive psychological influences of design include: good street lighting so we know where we are and who else is around; a dividing line between public and private space to signal what intrusion is; well-maintained places to reduce a feeling of things being out of control; good sight-lines so people can see what's going on; communal areas that encourage social interaction and walkability. These all relate to basic psychological needs, similar to a kind of Feng Shui of the neighbourhood, and seem to be more important than specific design styles. However, some design styles have impacted negatively.

Buenos Aires: We see in La Boca the human need even to beautify tin shacks and invest them with meaning.

Modernist planning, design and architecture influenced many post-war developments – some positively – but often had a harmful effect particularly on high-rise housing, with an overly rigid minimalist focus on separating functions and reducing complexity. Le Corbusier, in many ways a brilliant architect, developed the concept of houses as 'machines for living' which influenced these designs. He had a difficult relationship with his parents, married an alcoholic and has been described as a monomaniac narcissist with a violent temper. Should we read the resulting housing as a means of trying to regain control from his personal chaos, so it carries this sense of emotional trauma within its mechanical fabric, lacking compassion, empathy, or the human-scale qualities of earlier periods, leaving an inhospitable coldness?

The history of city making is littered with design casualties, including failed utopias. Cities in the sky became squalid prisons, an architectural vanity that decimated social networks. The psychology of the architect or property developer can clearly impact on the people they design for, and using the principles of psychology to investigate the effects of design judgements we can ask whether they in fact actually like people. This is not only legitimate but necessary.

Modernist place making focused too much on the rational and too little on the emotional

53

Alain de Botton claimed that "architects (are) failing to convert an unconscious grasp of their own needs into reliable instructions for satisfying the needs of others.[66]" This, he argues, leads to the kinds of disasters all too frequently visible in the urban landscape, where "bad architecture is in the end as much a failure of psychology as it is of design", but also mean spiritedness and an obsession with cost-saving without understanding its consequences.

Psychology is equally important in understanding how institutions, governance and social structures operate, as it 'goes behind' human behaviours, asking from where they emanate. De Botton similarly goes behind beauty, suggesting that an aesthetically pleasing environment reminds us of our search for a life well-lived, for fulfilment and happiness, and even propels us towards it, a theme similarly picked up by Phillip Blond[67] in his work on a 'Community Right to Beauty'.

Bio-Urbanism[68] provides a scientific basis for the positive effects of urban design that reflect the geometry of biological structures and scale that people can easily connect with. Organic materials, maximum natural light, and vistas that allow you to stretch horizons are all ways in which design can play to a deep-seated sense of ease.

Neighbourhoods that work well can successfully mediate between the needs of the city and those of a smaller local community, with city centres, parks and public spaces as collective hubs. People that live in walkable, mixed-use neighbourhoods are more likely to know their neighbours, engage in social, voluntary or political activity and trust people around them[69]. This lifeless physical space then becomes a living place as it is imbued with meaning, and meaning in turn provides purpose.

The meaning invested in a place is less tangible than its design, but just as critical. Meaning in relation to environment is formed from memories, current experiences and the associations with a place, a person's interpretation of its physical structures and activities, a mass of small and large encounters, social networks and activities. Places can engender anxiety – even fear – when crime and drug use is high, so meaning here is negative. And places can change their meaning. Think of the favelas in Rio de Janeiro or Medellin once frightening and tense for those who lived there and definitely 'no-go' for those from outside; now changed by inspiring libraries like the Comuna 13's San Javier library or La Biblioteca España, shifting the focus to learning, being together and re-developing trust. This has transformed the psychology of the place and its residents.

Every city has specific places to which meaning is attached, places to come to and places to avoid. There are often invisible boundaries from one to the next and this can be sensed. Some are more obvious like Mostar's Bridge in Bosnia, one side Croats and the other side Serbs. Others are invisible, like slipping into a side street off Garden District in New Orleans and being grasped by uncertainty, even fear.

*Lublin: The past is ever present.
Images of murdered Jews re-
appear where they once lived.*

People invent or express meanings by creating traditions, as with the Notting Hill Carnival, or to subvert architectural intentions, for example with new buildings and structures becoming fondly named and adopted ('The Big Pants' TV building in Beijing), or vilified ('Muggers Paradise' previously in Elephant and Castle, London).

The original purpose of a development or its designers' intention may have little to do with what is projected onto it by a community. A casual observer might perceive a new, highly successful and well-designed retail space, but sections of the local community could see it as 'not for us' or the place where they work long hours for low pay.

A deeper psychological and also cultural understanding will help us foresee how a development might be received by engaging with people at an emotional level as well as by asking 'how does it look and what does it do'. Incorporating these insights into the planning and consultation repertoire could pick up challenges before they become a problem.

Applied psychology has a clear and distinct role in helping us to understand more about how to create physical environments that satisfy human needs. In doing so, we can begin to design places with a purpose: to help people live better – emotionally and physically – healthier lives, and feel that this place 'is also for us'.

THE SOUL OF THE CITY

The Urban Psyche

'Soul' an unfashionable word perhaps, is frequently used regarding cities. A place is soulless or soul-full; we talk of the 'heart', 'life' of a city and that it has 'spirit' or is 'animated', both words that mean 'it breathes'. It is more than a lifeless being. We easily use emotive language or ethereal words for places and it reinforces the principle theme of this book — that the city is primarily an emotional experience. It shows people find more in cities than just its physical surface. The emotions of places are significant and equally as relevant as hard-edged measurements.

The filter of human experience conditions our perception and so without effort we see places as lived entities. Going with the grain of our innate tendency to 'humanise' and 'personify', we can begin conversations from a different starting point rather than conventional ways of talking about cities as inert. This is why we developed the City Personality Test as a means of instigating a new dialogue in cities across differing disciplines.

What is in this 'breath' of a city that we can feel, and which the city expresses itself from its inner core? It is the culture, character and personality which citizens share. We talk of the qualities we think of as Parisian, Glaswegian or Amsterdammer as if they were a person. The same is true for neighbourhoods. That place north or south of the river, or at the east or west end, the right or wrong side of the tracks. Cities, of course, have layered and complex cultural identities and to stereotype is reductive. Yet the link between city and communal identity is apparent since it is shaped by people.

The connection between city and individual identity and development is less visible, but no less real. As discussed, Place Identity and Place Attachment[70] theories demonstrate the strong link between a person's individual development and living environments. General well-being aside, it can determine the development of an individual's psychological and neurological functioning, particularly during childhood. This can have deep

Mexico City: The endless search for community in cities that can be anonymous.

and lasting impacts across a person's life. Our minds are literally shaped by our cities.

The psychologist and urbanist James Hillman, mentioned previously, suggests our relationship with cities can improve longer-term if we allow ourselves to think of them as having a real sense of animation independent from us, a 'personality' or sense of communal soul which has an inner energy or intensity. Hillman contrasts the modern treatment of the environment with ancient cultures that had a belief in animism. He notes that ancient people would find it unthinkable to treat the environment as detached and lifeless, as modern society frequently does.

... new solutions are possible if we see cities as having a sense of independent animation and personality

The future of cities will not rely on returning to a simplistic notion of animism. Instead Hillman's powerful analysis suggests that feeling the pulse of a city can help us change our relationship to it and he introduces the possibility that: "the entire ... model with which psychotherapy works – psychodynamics, psychopathology, the unconscious and even personality itself – might also apply to the world and its things."[1]"

Separating people from place, culture and their social and political contexts, results in "highly aware individuals and unconscious citizens". Instead, Hillman argues, seeing people as being at the centre of place and culture would shift many mistaken policy interventions – including some from psychology such as one-dimensional happiness indices.

He suggests, for instance, that depression or anxiety resulting from a lack of intimacy in formative parental relationships might be mirrored by planners, designers, architects or property developers creating cityscapes that lack that sense of intimacy and connection with its citizens, leading them to feel similarly insecure.

This resonates with the 'Peace Psychologists' (see Schools of Psychology and their Urban Potential' above) who noticed, while supporting negotiations in disputed territories, that if basic human psychological needs were not met then a solution was less likely.

Thinking about a whole city can feel abstract and overwhelming. By transferring the processes of psychology from people to cities, seeing them almost as if they were a person provides a fresh outlook and can place complex issues into a more understandable human perspective. This thinking leaves the importance of more

traditional urban policy intact but adds an extra insight by taking us into a landscape of feeling and emotion, humanising urban policy in a way which could have practical uses.

The Sacred City

An association between a sense of the sacred or divine and the city is quite ancient, seen in place names and urban legends. Suggesting that cities might have a personality or sense of communal spirit would not have seemed radical in the past.

Early cities tried to shrink the world around them, containing and controlling its random chaos. The farm and hunt become the grain store and market, a sacred landscape becomes a temple. Life previously spread out across vast landscapes and semi-nomadic existences could be controlled and structured in the highly efficient receptacle that is the city.

City walls keep in as well as keep out, and ironically, by walling themselves up the first city dwellers became the freest, most protected people on the planet. Then cities could act as accelerators of human ability and achievement.

The same process applied to religion and faith where by creating urban shrines and temples the gods were dragged from the

... cities close us in, yet can open us out to possibilities

Bristol: Sanctum by Theaster Gates.
In a bombed out church a stream of
visitors speak about their lives.

rivers, hills and the sky into the heart of the city itself, which then became a kind of 'spiritual mezzanine level' between people and their deities[72]. These special spaces looked inward, and were often hidden, guarded places. Connecting people to this realm through communal acts of worship and festival was crucial, making the whole of the city a sacred landscape and spiritual theatre.

Mythical city founders can be seen as a collective personification of the psyche of the city, made by its citizens over time in a way that represented their own values and beliefs. A sacred origin to a place is also clearly intended to stake a claim to its continued importance, its divine origins conferring reflected glory.

The dead were also important as many of the first cities were founded near necropoli, burial grounds of nomadic peoples who would return for festival and worship, eventually putting down roots – the wandering living perhaps envious of the settled dead.

Cities are often named after their divine founders or patrons – Rome, Athens, Los Angeles, Sao Paulo – seeming somehow to shape their destiny with great cathedrals, mosques, synagogues and other places of worship to celebrate them. Athens was founded on the spot of a battle between Poseidon, god of the oceans and Athena, goddess of wisdom. The Athenians became revered for their learning and wisdom. Rome was founded by

Romulus, twin son (with Remus whom he slew) of Mars the Roman god of war. Mars became the patron god of Rome, its early citizens known for their war-like nature, love of conquest and martial skill. Leicester is named for King Leir, and his legendary father Bladdud, is said to have founded Bath.

Location and design can also be mystically inspired. When caliph Al-Mansur founded Baghdad in 762 he used the horoscope to ensure the best possible moment for his new capital's inauguration, employing a committee of astrologers from various countries from across the known world. Mexico City was founded in 1325 on the spot in the middle of a lake where it was foreseen an eagle would land on a cactus. Rather more recently, Saltburn in Yorkshire was started in 1861 by Henry Pease (founder of the Stockton to Darlington railway) following a vision in which he saw the Divine City of the Book of Revelations, now reflected in Saltburn's layout and street names. Several building-patterns and structures in present-day Dubai are influenced by sacred Arabic geometry.

This arcane connection between faith and city suggests something else, that cities were for a long time seen as a kind of sacred object in themselves, and therefore city-making a sacred act. Psychological awareness might help recapture a similar sense of special purpose and meaning in city-making so triggering ways of thinking to make cities more viscerally connected to our deeper sources of motivation.

Urban policy should be secular but we should not deny the search for spirit and soul

The role of faith in the history of cities is more significant than simple curiosity. Religious and cultural tensions play out largely in urban settings, and are a critical component in grasping the dynamics of a city. Policy should be secular, but that does not mean there is no role for belief.

Faith leaders have been influential in finding solutions, from Northern Ireland to the Middle East. If faith groups within a city were to think more explicitly about the whole of urban policy including the symbolisms unearthed by psychology it could stimulate new thinking beyond individual religious or cultural silos. If the secular too could broaden their perspective through elements of urban psychology, together they might find more common ground to create better places to live, and new strategies for how they can collectively achieve this.

THE CITY PERSONALITY TEST

Psychology provides a number of tools to analyse people that could be applied to place, and we wondered what would happen if a city could take a personality test.

Would it be extrovert or introvert, sensitive or bullish, nurturing or selfish? What might it tell us about its strengths and weaknesses?

We started by adapting Myers Briggs, a well-known personality test used widely in employment assessment and psychology more generally. It produces sixteen different possible readouts or personality types, with names like Controller, Explorer, Accountant. We took this test and re-wrote it as if the city were a person. 'I like parties, celebrations and fancy dress' became 'My city likes celebrations, festivals and dressing itself up for special events'.

Myers Briggs uses four scales of measurement based on Jung's work: Introvert – Extrovert; Sensing – Intuition; Thinking - Feeling; Judgement – Perception. We soon realised the limitations of this method and that it was a little reductive and missed out some of the richer texture for something as complex as a city.

We then developed our own method linked to a web programme that could assimilate all the results into one 'personality'. Then using a combination of web results and workshops we tried it out with eleven cites. In this prototyping phase with Ghent, Antwerp, Adelaide, Minneapolis, Milton Keynes, Mannheim, Krakow, Bilbao, Oslo, Plymouth and Cheltenham we gathered 400 plus responses from a variety of audiences including the young and the old, women and men and differing social groups. Typically, between 30-40 people participated, and we expected the results to be spread fairly evenly across the different personality types, thinking that if true it would still be useful in stimulating a debate. The early results were fascinating. Instead of an even spread, in each case 50% or more respondents' results showed the same or very similar personality types, with the remainder often clustered around two or three other personality types.

In the workshops with test participants, when we read the results out to people the effect was often electric. Not only did people

Muscat: Cities of shadow and light: A measured pattern created by the sun.

Lublin: A Hokusai imitation graffiti; a hopeful story of waves and organic flow on a dilapidated building.

recognise their city – although there were different views on the detail – they instantly engaged in discussion in an entirely different way to a more mainstream consultation.

It was as if they were talking about a neighbour, family member or even themselves. It opened up a new way of thinking and communicating about really complex issues within the city that can often get mired in technical detail and alienate. There was a liberating effect, people didn't have to know anything about planning, infrastructure, housing needs, they could just talk about how it felt to them, what the character and emotional impact of a place was, which totally absorbed them and lead to talking about how things might change.

The City Personality Test uses seven scales of measurement, which provide a potential 175 different 'personality' readouts capable of combining any number of responses into one median score. People can answer questions at one of five different points along each scale. This produces seven paragraphs of pre-written text per readout, and there is a section that focuses on strengths, weaknesses and possible strategies for a city to consider.

Introvert	Extrovert
Sensitive, self-sufficient, needs own space	Outgoing, thick skinned, party animal, cannot act alone
Nurturing	**Self-Absorbed**
Emotionally intelligent, caring, considered	Self-reflective, investigative, solitary, exploitative
Agreeable	**Disagreeable**
Charismatic, reliable, tries to please all	Speaks its mind, charmless, unreliable
Conscientious	**Spontaneous**
Ethical, tidy, planner, measured, collaborative	Exciting, passionate, chaotic, risk taker
Curious	**Driven**
Perceptive, open minded, tolerant, outward looking, procrastinates, knowledgeable	Focused, judgemental, goal-oriented, ambitious, decision taker, resourceful
Integrated	**Compartmentalised**
Authentic, team player, participative	Siloed, go it alone, detailed
Idealistic	**Practical**
Spiritual, has grand and charitable aims	Rational, task-oriented

Readers wishing to do the test can do so by logging into http://urbanpsyche.org where we have included most of the cities in the world. If yours is not included please contact enquiries@urbanpsyche.org and we will insert it. Results of the tests – where agreed with cities – appear on our web resource. A few tasters are included below, just extracts from the several pages of results the test provides. We stress these are people's perceptions, not our view or what the place necessarily 'is'.

Milton Keynes represents an idea bigger than itself, is altruistic, believes in volunteering help and is family-oriented. It is sensitive and can tend toward procrastination, but has a fun side and likes to throw a party. It has a sense of the aesthetic, but is also highly rational and can be seen as cold by those that don't know it.

The results of the urban psyche test create a new conversation

Adelaide has suffered from a lack of confidence that it is slowly regaining. It is beginning to feel at ease with itself, aware that it is not flashy and brash but more solid and paced and purposeful.

Bilbao is proud, perhaps even too proud, confident in its local identity, it feels it has a destiny, it is ambitious but realistic, entrepreneurial yet solid in how it goes about things.

Plymouth is an adventurous explorer, yet methodical and logical in its search for a sense of meaning, wanting to strengthen its identity. Its highly collaborative approach is positive, but can sometimes arise from a lack of self-reliance and confidence; it would sometimes just like to be told what to do.

Antwerp is free spirited and thrives on networks and contacts. It takes pride in improving the lives of others. It is precise and competent in its actions, dislikes laziness and is highly moral. It is entrepreneurial and determined, but can come across as dominating and unforgiving.

Minneapolis is a highly motivated and energetic place that enjoys a festival. Its good at supporting people's emotional needs, but doesn't always cut through to the root of a problem because it can be conflict-averse. It is great at coming up with new ideas, but not always at following them through into action.

Ghent has an air of natural and charismatic ease, a confident place that seeks to improve the wellbeing of people, but that sometimes takes on others' problems too deeply. It is a highly sociable and networked place, and although it has a strong grasp of logic, can let the heart rule the head, acting on intuition and coming up with complex solutions when something simpler would do.

This Test cannot currently be used as a scientific basis for assessing everything a city is or needs to do, but is incredibly useful to kick-start a conversation and to engage people, and, as it is further tested and refined, it can make better judgements and recommendations to a city. Its strength is that it mobilises our innate ability to humanise, allowing people to talk about the complexity of place as if it were a person, something everyone can relate to.

Future work will involve far larger samples in order to understand better the links between the personality type of the person taking the Test and their results. In particular, younger people and others often excluded from city strategies will be engaged to explore what correlations there are between demographic differences.

Another focus will be to use the Test with individual neighbourhoods as well as cities as it has enormous potential as a community planning and engagement tool. We are investigating how other tools from psychology can be applied to cities, for example a kind of psychoanalysis of the history and major life events of a city's past and what that might reveal about its present and future potentials.

Helsinki: There is no such thing as a typical city resident.

THE PSYCHOLOGICALLY RESILIENT CITY

Concern with a city's psychology is not an exercise in psycho-babble, but part of a search for better explanations of how cities work, the effects they have on people and how we can improve them.

How we feel in different places – particularly where we grow up, live and work – conditions our sense of self, our levels of energy, aspirations, our commitment to others and our sense of community; in short, our entire state of wellbeing.

Imagine a lifetime spent in the worst possible urban environment. How does it make you feel, what potential and possibility does it offer? Now imagine the best.

There is, as noted, a rich history of exploration by thinkers and commentators on what makes people feel emotionally and psychologically secure in cities. Yet the obvious common threads of this work have not been drawn together in a comprehensive way, begging the question: if we know all this, why have we not done something about it?

There are admirable efforts, starting in different places (the built environment, health, happiness indices) pointing toward the same destination. The time has come for this agenda.

To Improve Yourself, You Improve Your City

The drive toward wholeness and integration as a process of reaching maturity is a basic principle of most branches of psychology – often found in faiths as well. Jung called this Individuation, the Italian psychiatrist Roberto Assagioli psychosynthesis and others have differing names. What is commonly held is that psychological maturity and development is based on self-knowledge and the ability to balance the internal dynamics that create a sense of being individual within a healthy relationship to community.

Venice: 'The Key in Hand' by Chiharu Shiota. The boat, the yarn and 2000 keys unlock our journeys through life.

In the context of the city we might describe this as 'psychological resilience', the ability of a place to adapt, deal with adversity and complexity, to bounce back and continue to function competently, and to provide the conditions in which its inhabitants can achieve those outcomes too.

It is a radical idea to conceive of place-making and management as grounded in a broader understanding of human psychology, which will enable us to flourish psychologically. Can the places we inhabit help us develop as whole human beings, or at the very least, get less in the way? Hillman states:

"How we imagine our cities, how we envision their goals and values and enhance their beauty defines the self of each person in that city, for the city is the solid exhibition of the communal soul. This means that you find yourself by entering the crowd ... to improve yourself you improve your city."

This implies decision makers at all levels recognizing the power and impact of psychology and feeling comfortable to explore its insights, interpretations and sources of knowledge. This means going beyond wellbeing surveys and happiness indices and imagining an enriched citizenship and set of empathic civic values embedded in our institutions and governance. Cities that offer people space to grow and to harness psychological resources towards personal and community development and fulfilment. A business as usual approach will not work. Cities that achieve this will become more successful and sustainable places to live.

... "the city is the solid exhibition of the communal soul"

Carol Ryff summarizes[73] six measures that provide people with psychological resilience, developed as they mature. They are: how people are making use of their personal talents and potential (personal growth); the depth of connection they had in ties with significant others (positive relationships); whether they viewed themselves to be living in accord with their own personal convictions, in essence being themselves (autonomy); how well they were managing their life situations (environmental mastery); the extent to which people feel their lives have meaning, purpose, and direction (purpose in life); and the knowledge and acceptance they had of themselves, including awareness of personal limitations (self-acceptance).

Simplistic conclusions are difficult because individual reactions to different interventions will depend on your sense of identity, cultural background, stage in life, what you want or need, your mood. What people want can also seem contradictory and may switch; stimulation and vitality at one moment to calmness and tranquillity at the next, and the 'good' city tries to cater for all. Yet

Frankfurt: Random acts of kindness foster generosity and create civility

there are underlying patterns of psychological need that people hold in common, and they all require a physical or atmospheric expression in order to create psychologically resilient cities.

A Toolkit for Psychologically Resilient Cities

Drawing together the common threads we have unearthed in our own exploration, six similar major psychological themes become apparent, each of which has particular significance within cities, contributing toward the psychological resilience of a place and its people. These themes do not replace other priorities (like employment for example), but are things that matter to our well-being from our earliest moments onward (and that jobs alone cannot provide). It is useful to consider the extent to which any city can provide these conditions.

1. **The possibility for improvement (personal growth)**: The conditions for achieving people's potential, growing toward a sense of ease, fulfilment and completeness. Does the city display empathy in its practices, does it exhibit a concrete sense of wanting everyone to do well, with programmes that match that aspiration? Is it a place where people are able to feel that anything is possible? Are basic wellbeing factors catered for to encourage:

... to what extent do cities nurture our psychological needs?

connection; activity; curiosity; learning; giving?

2. **The ability to deal with difference and find connection (positive relationships):** positively experiencing diversity, embracing complexity as enrichment, building communal trust and social capital. Does the city operate interculturally, are there activities and events that encourage communities to bond and to mix, and to share in a collective sense of the cities identity? Is social media and the networks they create fully exploited in the interests of communal wellbeing? Is the city able to get to the root causes of conflict and deal with them? Are neighbourhoods designed and run in a way that maximises wellbeing and social capital, does the layout create interactions, walkability, build trust? Do the social institutions of the city mirror these values?

3. **Places that reflect the courage of their convictions (autonomy):** encountering places that are locally authentic, reflect aspiration and a value set. Is design delivering excellence in the everyday just as much as the iconic buildings? What are the values of the city and how are these reflected in its place-making? Is there an attempt to evaluate the psychological impacts of design decisions? Is the purpose of a housing block a roof over the head, or does it reflect a deeper mission, helping people to live well? Do the conditions to create positive Place Attachment and Place Identity exist?

4. **Nurturing deep-seated needs (environmental mastery):** having easy access to facilities and an environment that meet basic human needs, including natural resources and quiet space. Is there an explicit understanding of human environmental needs and a strategy to meet these? Do neighbourhoods have a high quality of amenities, and are they well-linked to bigger, city-wide cultural and social assets? Are there events that cyclically mark the passing of time, and places where a sense of time can be lost? Does the city actively to seek to enable the following psychological requirements: feeling secure; belonging; self-esteem and respect; a right to cultural identity; an ability to participate; and a sense of fairness?

There is an emerging consensus as to what makes us feel at ease and whole

5. **Self-awareness, knowing where the city wants to go, and driven to help others (purpose in life):** awareness of strengths and weaknesses, an explicit plan for a better future and a desire to help everyone share in it. Does the city understand the

Venice: Proportio by Axel Vervoordt and Daniela Ferretti explores the omnipresence of universal proportions in art, science, music and architecture.

psychological Impacts of its history, its major 'life-events' and geography (a kind of self-psychoanalysis)? Is there an awareness of how others see it, not just how it wants to be seen? Does it have a strong, visible and shared narrative for its future rooted in local identity and culture? Could it be described as generous, compassionate, a place that is here to help?

6. **Balancing citizenship, self and community (self-acceptance)**: creating a sense of citizenship that balances the rights, responsibilities, social requirements and the identity of the city with those of different communities and individuals. Is active citizenship encouraged and given the tools to express itself? Do people understand what their rights and obligations are, does the leadership of the city reflect the values of citizenship they encourage in others (like 'Whole Place Leadership' — a concept developed by the Core Cities UK)? Do citizens feel listened to and valued? Is there a kind of a 'social contract' between the city and the individual (behaviours that are expected, with opportunity and support given in return)? Are different cultural identities actively validated in a way that encourages participation in the life of the city as a whole? Does the city feel like a place happy in its own skin, not comparing itself to others all the time?

Seoul: A symbol of civic generosity in Dongdaemun Design Plaza by Zaha Hadid.

Shifting any city toward psychological resilience begins with a series of questions, partly about how its performance stacks up against these six guidelines, but against other less tangible measures too. For example, is the experience of the city unified rather than fragmented, secure rather than uncertain?

... bland sameness can becalm but an incoherent approach to variety can feel messy

Diversity and the excitement of difference can seem at odds with a sense of calm, but is profoundly important to cities, in terms of communities as well as buildings, activities and visual complexity. Does a city offer the variety that attracts and maintains a creative milieu, animating the senses, stimulating the imagination and generating creativity and innovation?

Whilst bland sameness can becalm a city, an incoherent approach to variety can feel messy or precarious – even chaotic and difficult – to absorb. Some cultures feel bright lights are comforting and others that it inundates the senses. When we are insecure we hanker after the familiar, when we are secure the new is less threatening.

Balancing the different components of a psychologically resilient city is therefore critical, relating to what is deemed right in that context, although we should recognise our judgements are not value free. Some places seem to exude only their past, some aspirations for their future. We might experience narrow sidewalks next to looming buildings that overwhelm us, little if any greenery, low quality materials, few panoramas, nowhere to sit, car fumes. Or instead we might feel inspired by shape, form, colour and materials, extraordinary everyday buildings, quality green and pedestrian spaces. As Colin Ellard notes, a sense of intrigue in the physical environment is "a matter of public health – mental health in particular" and instinctively we are all good urban designers. Boring landscapes increase levels of debilitating stress, whereas enriched surroundings broaden our capacities. We are biologically driven to want to be in places with interest and complexity.

The city communicates through every fibre of its being, its physical and social structures, governance, its life and animation. These things combine in a powerful way that impacts directly upon the psychology of its people, which in turn impact on place, so creating a cycle: an urban psychology.

Oscar Wilde said that most of the ugly things around us were made by someone trying to create something beautiful, whilst most of the beautiful things were made by someone trying to make something that worked. Beauty and ugliness in a city are highly subjective, but generally we know what does and does not work for us. Urban design and architecture have, to a large extent, fathomed what makes this so, but the built environment is not the city, it is only an expression of it.

Urban psychology helps us to see the city also as a social stage, where we have to encounter strangers, transact, exchange and share. The city thus needs to create the conditions where positive encounters happen and social capital is built. Social connections are as important to our survival as food, safety, and shelter. Our brains are socially wired, notes Lieberman[74] "When neuroscientists monitor what's going on in someone's brain, they are typically interested in what happens in it when people are involved in an active task,... and our default network directs us to think about other people's minds – their thoughts, feelings, and goals. Whenever it has a free moment, the human brain has an automatic reflex to go social." Connecting with others, especially when you know they need your help, even in the simplest ways makes you happier, with a calculable monetary value.[75][76]

The city communicates emotionally through every fibre of its being

London: A sign in Olympic Park in 2012.

The desire for and necessity of community has not changed with the rise of the digital world, but how it is expressed and is socially constructed has. It is less bound to the fixed physical spaces of traditional community. Coupled with the astonishing technical advances that have enabled us to move and be mobile, this allows a more nomadic way of life within which we can affiliate and identify ourselves in multiple ways. Networks can define community more than traditional bonds in a technologically nomadic world, and cities must also adapt and understand how these networks can be brought to bear for the psychological benefit of a place and its people.

Tensions between the wider social needs of the city as a whole and the tribal play themselves out in the city, its sharpest expressions being visible and invisible ghettoes, based on interests, tight relations, prejudices and culture. People look for and choose the like-minded for convenience, to avoid the complexity of mutual understanding or to feel safer, creating in-group thinking and excluding difference as a default position. This dynamic has a strong flip side in cities, those who enjoy the delights of difference, freeing up their exploratory instinct, the urban nomad or tourist. Here the digitized world has escalated the capacity to form networks of connection with relative freedom. The

collective urban experience thus takes on an added importance. With fragmented communication channels the norm and tribal affiliation growing, there are fewer common events to be discussed over the clichéd water cooler. This is why festivals, culture, sporting and spectacular events frame an increasingly significant part of urban culture.

This all is encapsulated in a feeling of does this place say "yes or no". The "yes" city will have an enabling spirit of generosity, openness and a welcoming attitude. Beyond a city meeting the basic necessities of life, what this boils down to is the ability to: feel a sense of anchorage and the familiar; experience the possibilities of choice, options and a 'can do' atmosphere; connect with others, the wider world and successfully deal with differences; successfully manage and move on from conflict; engross oneself for either distraction or self-improvement; and lift out of the day-to-day grind into a different, higher level of experience.

Mexico City: Invasive advertising being taken over by art works.

WHERE NEXT FOR URBAN PSYCHOLOGY

It is abundantly clear that urban psychology has much to offer in understanding how to make and manage places so they can impact positively on our wellbeing, helping us to live richer, more fulfilling lives.

It also has significant potential in developing a toolkit to build-in psychological resilience, not just to the built forms of a city but to its social structures, institutions and governance.

Living together with our differences in relative harmony and with a sense of fairness and justice remains the central challenge of our time. It is part of a global agenda being addressed with increasing urgency and one where urban psychology can add immense value.

Yet, with some respectable exceptions, the resources offered across the fields of psychology lie almost dormant in respect of cities, and we should urgently mobilise these to the benefit of cities and citizens. To repeat, we can see three distinct levels of application of urban psychology:

1. **Perception and connection:** Refreshing our ways of seeing and connecting with the city at a human, emotional level, unlocking new solutions and avenues of exploration for residents and policy makers. The City Personality Test is an example.

2. **Psychologically aware city-making:** Providing a new toolkit for use alongside more conventional strategies for how we develop and plan cities, not just for urban form and functions, but for wellbeing, social and economic policies to help a city succeed for the long term; to create psychologically resilient cities.

3. **Specific interventions:** Calling on the resources of psychology to generate a set of tailored interventions, through research which seeks to apply psychological models to specific urban issues: health; community engagement; transport; climate change or welfare to work programmes.

Hazrat Nizamuddin, Delhi: Psychology is not a panacea, but has untapped potential.

This agenda is internationally significant and worth serious consideration by agencies like UN Habitat and the World Health

Belfast City Hall: The physical fabric fosters civic togetherness.

Organisation as well as national bodies and locally. Agencies whose remit includes health, cities, or both should come together in an international dialogue on urban psychology, asking specific questions, based on the framework we have set out. The aim should be to create a long-term research agenda, but also to generate new, practical solutions for urban issues. This should include: looking at interactions of individuals and groups in the city; the built, institutional and social structures of the city; and civic values and citizenship.

... we are only at the beginning of understanding what makes humans tick

Work is definitely required in how to more clearly assess wellbeing and what it precisely means. Building on existing work, national bodies, such as the UK Office of National Statistics, could take a lead. Internationally the current models do not go deep enough and are rarely located at the level of the city. Cities need to know more about how they are doing and what levers they can apply to create improvements.This has implications for national policy decisions too, as those levers need to be in the hands of cities, not national governments.

The City Personality Test will be constant work in progress, getting refined as new insights, ideas or applications surface. We hope the tool will be widely used by cities and neighbourhoods to begin conversations from a different starting point and to realise novel solutions. In parallel we are actively exploring how other psychological tools can be translated from person to place so enriching the Toolkit for Psychologically Resilient Cities.

Longer term this agenda needs an institutional champion to drive it forward and act as a repository for new thinking. Organised along multidisciplinary lines, a kind of 'Bauhaus for Place' is needed, which seeks to do for the whole city what the original did for individual objects and buildings. Revolutionising how we investigate the complexity of the whole built and socio-economic urban landscape, with psychologists, economists, sociologists, anthropologists, as well as designers, artists and planners involved. One aim should be to influence the training and development of those professionally involved with cities, bringing in urban psychology. Creating a new institution is important, but places can pick this up now, and in a digital age, an institution does not necessarily need walls to get going or to develop learning programmes.

This embedding process is similar to what happened when feminism or environmental thinking was incorporated into urban practice. The question is always 'do we need a specific person' to highlight the issues or should awareness spread throughout an organisation. We need both, however, with psychology there are so many schools and so we need to ensure that its broad spectrum is acknowledged rather than only using, say, insights from the behaviourist school.

Our aim more than anything has been to stimulate a debate about cities from a different direction to get at new solutions and, whether people agree or disagree, we welcome contact, contributions and ideas. The future of our species is now closely linked to cities, and the lens of urban psychology brings valuable insight into how we can best realise a successful future for both.

Urban psychology offers enormous potential to transform existing cities and the way we interact with them. It can help us to create future places within which we can live more at ease, both with each other and with the place itself, in a way that will have a positive impact on individual and community health, life quality, life chances, the economy, and on how public and private services are shaped.

REFERENCES

[1] Urban Stress and Mental Health; Mazda Adli; November 2011; LSE Cities

[2] Westminster Lecture for Samaritans; 'Working together to reduce suicide in transport'; December 2015

[3] Psyche and the City: A Souls Guide to the Modern Metropolis; Singer, T; Eds; Spring Journal Inc; New Orleans; 2010

[4] http://charleslandry.com/panel/wp-content/themes/twentyeleven/books/The-Creative-City-Index.pdf

[5] Psyche and the City: A Souls Guide to the Modern Metropolis; Singer, T; Eds; Spring Journal Inc; New Orleans; 2010

[6] Containing Tensions: Psychoanalysis and modern policy making; Cooper, A; in Juncture; IPPR; London; Vol 22, 2015.

[7] The World Outside Your Head: on becoming an individual in an age of distraction; Crawford, M.B; Farrar, Straus and Giroux; New York; 2015

[8] The Routledge Handbook of Embodied Cognition; Shapiro, L; Eds; 2014

[9] Thinking, Fast and Slow; Kahneman, D; Penguin; London; 2011

[10] Gestalt Principles; how are your designs perceived? http://vanseodesign.com/web-design/gestalt-principles-of-perception/

[11] Healing the Inner City Child: Creative Arts Therapies with At-Risk Youth; Camilleri, V. A; Eds; Jessica Kingsley Publishers; London; 2007 [12] https://positivepsychologyprogram.com/founding-fathers/

[13] http://www.positivedisintegration.com/positivepsychology.htm [14] http://mythosandlogos.com/Hillman.htmlphorical

[15] The World Outside Your Head: on becoming an individual in an age of distraction; Crawford, M.B; Farrar, Straus and Giroux; New York; 2015 [16] Dawkins, R; 1976

[17] Opening Skinners Box: Great Psychological Experiments of the Twentieth Century; Slater, L; Bloomsbury Publishing; 2005 [18] Milgram, S; The Experience of Living in Cities; Science; 1970

[19] Kelman, H; Conflict Resolution and Reconciliation: A Social-Psychological Perspective on Ending Violent Conflict Between Identity Groups; 2011

[20] Social Capital and Diversity, Some Lessons from Canada; Kazemipur, A; Peter Laing; 2009

[21] The Brain is not Computable; Regalado, A; MIT Technology Review; 18.02.2013

[22] Places of the Heart: the Psychogeography of Everyday Life; Ellard, C; Bellvue Literary Press; 2015

[23] The Psychogeographic Review; Seal, B; 14/11/2013 [24] Psychogeography; Self, W and Steadman R; Bloomsbury; 2013

[25] http://nws.eurocities.eu/MediaShell/media/EUROCITIES%20stmt_smarter%20cities_May%202015_FINAL.pdf

[26] Urban Psychology; its history and current status; Journal of Social Distress and the Homeless; Vol 14; 2005

[27] http://bcep2015.nl/

[28] Report of the Task Force on Urban Psychology: Toward an Urban Psychology; Research, Action and Policy (APA 2005) https://www.apa.org/pi/ses/resources/publications/urban-taskforce.pdf

[29] Wakefield, J; BBC News website; 27/08/13 [30] Readers Digest; October 2013

[31] Glaiser, E; Gottlieb, J. D; Ziv, O; Unhappy Cities; National Bureau of Economic Research; US; 2014

[32] Kunstler, J.H; The City in Mind: Meditations on the Urban Condition; The Free Press; New York; 2003

[33] Washington Population Statistics Bureau? [34] State of the Worlds Cities; UN Habitat; 2008-9

[35] McCay, L; Centre for Urban Design and Mental Health; http://www.urbandesignmentalhealth.com/

[36] MacLean, Paul D. (1990). The triune brain in evolution: role in paleocerebral functions. New York: Plenum Press

[37] How Many Friends does One Person Need?; Dunbar, R; Faber; 2010 [38] Hillman, J; Soul and the City

[39] Bazalgette, P; The Empathy Instinct: A Blueprint for Civil Society; 2017

[40] Bishop, B; The Big Sort: Why the Clustering of Like Minded America is Tearing us Apart; 2008

[41] http://www.tedcantle.co.uk/publications/012%20The%20end%20of%20parallel%20lives%20the%202nd%20Cantle%20Report%20Home%20Off.pdf

[42] https://www.gov.uk/government/publications/the-casey-review-a-review-into-opportunity-and-integration

[43] Johnson, R. A; Owning Your Own Shadow; The Dark Side of the Psyche; Harper; 1991

[44] https://sites.google.com/site/londonmoodapp/home

[45] The World Beyond Your Head: How to Flourish in an Age of Distraction; Crawford, M; 2015; Viking

[46] The Flâneur, the Badaud, and the Making of a Mass Public in France, circa 1860–1910; Shaya, G; American Historical Review 109; 2004

[47] A Geography of Time: The Temporal Misadventures of a Social Psychologist or How Every Culture Keeps Time Just a Little Bit Differently, Robert V. Levine, Basic Books 1998

[48] Time Warped: Unlocking the Mysteries of Time Perception by Claudia Hammond Harper Perennial, 2013

[49] The Rise of the Creative Class; Florida, R; 2002

[50] http://worldhappiness.report/wp-content/uploads/sites/2/2016/03/HR-V1_web.pdf

[51] The Discovery of Happiness, ed. Stuart McReady, Sourcebooks, 2001 https://papers.ssrn.com/sol3/papers.cfm?abstract_id=2168436   [52] file:///C:/Users/Charles/Downloads/RP2119.pdf

[53] http://www.theatlantic.com/health/archive/2013/08/meaning-is-healthier-than-happiness/278250/

[54] Soft City: A Psychological Handbook for Urban Survival; Raban, J; 1974; Picador

[55] http://www.huffingtonpost.com/2013/12/15/psychology-materialism_n_4425982.html

[56] https://www.theguardian.com/commentisfree/2016/may/17/money-cant-buy-happiness-wishful-thinking

[57] https://www.thersa.org/action-and-research/rsa-projects/public-services-and-communities-folder/inclusive-growth-commission

[58] Happy City; Montgomery, C; 2014; Farrar, Straus & Giroux

[59] http://neweconomics.org/five-ways-to-wellbeing-the-evidence/?_sft_project=five-ways-to-wellbeing

[60] Stress recovery during exposure to natural and urban environments, Roger Ulrich et al .Journal of Environmental Psychology (1991)

[61] https://www.fig.net/resources/proceedings/fig_proceedings/fig2012/papers/ts06h/TS06H_cellmer_senetra_et_al_5748.pdf

[62] Piff, P. K. et al; Awe, the Small Self, and Prosocial Behavior; APA; Journal of Personality and Social Psychology; 2015

[63] http://www.spacesyntax.com/   [64] International Academy for Design and Health; designandhealth.com

[65] McKay,L; The Centre for Urban Design and Mental Health

[66] The Architecture of Happiness; Alain de Botton; 2008

[67] Respublica; 2015   [68] Caperna, A; A New Paradigm for Deep Sustainability: Biourbanism; 2014

[69] Leyden, K.M; Am J Public Health; 2003 September; 93(9): 1546-1551

[70] Harold Proshansky, Abbe Fabian, and Robert Kaminoff; Place-Identity; 1983

[71] City and Soul: Hillman, J; 2006; Spring Publications, Connecticut

[72] The City in History; Mumford, L; 1961; Harbinger, New York

[73] https://www.psychologytoday.com/blog/theory-knowledge/201405/six-domains-psychological-well-being and http://midus.wisc.edu/findings/pdfs/830.pdf

[74] Social: Why Our Brains Are Wired to Connect; Mathew D. Lieberman; 2013; Crown

[75] Processing power limits social group size: computational evidence for the cognitive costs of sociality; T. Dávid-Barrett, R. I. M. Dunbar; 2013; Proceedings of the Royal Society B

[76] http://www.theatlantic.com/health/archive/2013/10/social-connection-makes-a-better-brain/280934/

ACKNOWLEDGEMENTS

Margie Caust, Urban Thinker & Adviser, Adelaide

Geoff Snelson, Director of Strategy, Milton Keynes Council

Idoia Postigo, Head of External Relations Bilbao Metropoli 30 and founder 'The Emotional Factory'

Karl-Filip Coenegrachts, Chief Strategy Officer, Ghent

Annelore Raman, Strategy Co-ordination, Ghent

Kris Achten and Stéphanie Lacocque, Enterprise and City Marketing, Antwerp

Einar Sneve Martinussen, Associate Professor and Coordinator of Interaction Design at the Oslo School of Architecture and Design

Dominic Jinks, Director of Plymouth Culture

Justyna Jochym, Head of Development and International Co-operation, Krakow Festivals Office

Mark VanderSchaaf, former Regional Planning Director, Metropolitan Council of Minneapolis-Saint Paul

Julie Finch, Director Cheltenham Trust

Rainer Kern, Director UNESCO City of Music, Mannheim

Francesca Froy, Urban Researcher

... and especially **Jonathan Hyams** who developed the website for the City Personality Test and edited the book.

'Increasingly cities should focus on what really drives human desires and needs and I am really pleased Charles and Chris have put the psychological perspective onto the city making agenda.'

Tina Saaby, City Architect of Copenhagen

'I wish I had written this book. Its message is overdue. Past approaches have mostly failed to produce the urban living environments we need to thrive. Applying urban psychology ambitiously and responsively will provide homo urbanis with meaningful places for living that can support urban thrival and psychological wellbeing.'

Professor Rhiannon Corcoran, Academic Director of the Heseltine Institute for Public Policy & Practice: Health & Well-Being, University of Liverpool, UK. Director, What Works Centre for Wellbeing, Community Wellbeing Evidence Programme.

TITLES IN THE SERIES

The Comedia Shorts series are all available from: **www.charleslandry.com**